D1104081

Forget Them Not

Forget Them Not

A Holistic Guide to Prison Ministry

JOANNE HEMENWAY

FOREWORD BY HOWARD ZEHR

WIPF & STOCK · Eugene, Oregon

FORGET THEM NOT
A Holistic Guide to Prison Ministry

Wipf & Stock
An Imprint of Wipf and Stock Publishers
199 W. 8th Ave., Suite 3
Eugene, OR 97401
www.wipfandstock.com

ISBN 978-1-60899-320-8

Manufactured in the U.S.A.

www.wipfandstock.com

Biblical quotations are from the New Revised Standard Version

Contents

Foreword

THE CHRISTIAN CHURCH HAS a long history of responding to Jesus' call to minister to prisoners. Given the alarming number of prisoners in this country, many of whom will return to our communities, this ministry desperately needs to be expanded.

Joanne Hemenway makes this case, as others have, but definitely goes much further: She reevaluates the conceptual and theological framework within which this ministry occurs and explores the social and historical context in which prisons are situated. She then goes on to outline three practical models of prison ministry grounded in this analysis.

This kind of background is essential but all too often missing from prison ministry literature. Indeed, much of the church's outreach to prisoners has been undertaken within an individualistic, vertical theology, often without a critical awareness of the underlying context of structural violence in which crime and punishment occurs. As a result, critics have charged that our ministries are at best a Band-Aid and at worst may perpetuate the cycle of violence and injustice.

Moreover, Christian ministries tend to be one-sided, rightly concerned about the needs of those who have offended but ignoring the needs of the "other side" of crime: those who have been harmed by crime. This neglect of victims parallels the way the justice system itself sidelines victims and is rooted in history.

The early Christian church understood wrongdoing as harm to people and relationships. This understanding was shaped by the guiding vision that God offers us: to live in *shalom*, that is, in right relationship with others, with God, and with creation. As Matthew 18 implies, making things right with our sisters and brothers is part of making things right with God. Zaacheus certainly understood that salvation required him to address the harms he had done.

In a provocative essay, Julian Pleasants has argued that the church, paralleling developments in the western legal system, eventually moved away from its historical stance. Like the legal system, it has come to define wrongdoing as broken rules, a violation of a higher authority, more than harm done to people. Rather than a violation of people that needed to be made right, offenses became sins against God, a God who increasingly came to be seen as a stern judge who would punish unless appeased.

From there it was a short step to the idea that salvation is obtained primarily by making things right with God in order to avoid punishment. We who offend are encouraged to seek forgiveness from and reconciliation with God—quick, before we are punished severely—while our obligations to human victims are minimized. Not surprisingly then, as a result, prison ministries often advise prisoners about how to experience forgiveness from God with little reference to their obligations to the people they have harmed.

In short, traditional Christianity has focused on the individual relationship between wrongdoer and God. In contrast, Pleasant notes, a core meaning of the cross is that God identifies with those who are hurting, whether victims or offenders. To regain this more holistic vision, Hemenway advocates a more relational approach to theology rooted in God's vision for the kingdom.

Again, Biblical justice envisions God's intention for humankind as a condition of shalom: a world in which people live in right relationship, a condition of "all-rightness." The wrong of crime is less that it breaks rules than it damages relationships, making the right relationships of shalom impossible. This understanding of wrongdoing is fundamental to the restorative justice approach that Hemenway suggests as an appropriate conceptual framework for our ministries.

As Hemenway says, the kingdom of God is not simply something for the future: we are called to work to build the kingdom, the "beloved community," here on earth. Empowerment and awareness, she argues, must be the cornerstones of a genuine prison ministry that helps to build this community. In the following pages she goes far to help build this foundation.

Howard Zehr
Professor of Restorative Justice
Center for Justice & Peacebuilding
Eastern Mennonite University, Virginia

Preface

Our sorry, idiot life, our idiot existence, idiot not because it has to be but because it is not what it could be with a little more courage and care.

—Thomas Merton, *A Year with Thomas Merton*

THE STORY OF RUTHIE

WITHIN EVERY HUMAN HEART there is longing—the yearning for love, for acceptance, and for mutual relation within the human family. Our lives originate from the most intimate of human connections, and the human life that springs forth is unique to all forms of life in its possibilities for consciousness, emotion, and awareness. Our growth, our well-being, our self-actualization are all deeply dependent on the quality of the human relationships that permeate our day to day, year to year, life-long living.

Some of us are very fortunate. We are born into families where there is mutual concern, caring, compassion for all family members. Parents themselves have had opportunities for a wealth of human experience, learning, education, and professions that enhance not only their own lives but their children's lives, and perhaps even the larger world as well. There is depth and richness to the quality of life.

On the far opposite end of the spectrum, however, are those who are least fortunate, those who are given little opportunity to grow into the fullness of their humanity. Perhaps they have not been wanted or welcomed. Perhaps their fate is such that their parents have been beaten down, ground under by poverty, by lack of education, by lack of opportunity, and by the vicissitudes of human suffering rooted in systemic and structural violence.

However, from the very best to the very worst and all the way in between, there is the complexity of the human person and the complexity of our human relationships. While in our scientific knowledge and technology we have made enormous advances, in the area of human living, in the area of our human consciousness and self-awareness, we are still in the dark ages. So often, we have little idea of what we are doing or why; we have little awareness of all the forces that shape us individually as well as together in relationship. All too often we are, as Jesus of Nazareth suggested, the blind leading the blind. We cannot see completely, we cannot know completely; we need all the help we can get each and every day of our lives. Nowhere is this truth more urgent than in the care and nurturing of children.

In his book, *Teachings on Love*, Zen master Thich Nhat Hanh states, "so many parents raise their children without mindfulness."[1] How well I know the truth of his words, for out of my own childhood experience I am keenly sensitive to the interactions of children and adults around me. As a child, one is powerless, vulnerable, completely at the mercy of the adults in his or her life. So many adults lack an understanding of the enormous power they carry in relationship to children and the vital necessity of mutual interaction with children through "relational power rather than power over."[2] Now, the reader might well ask, what has any of this to do with fostering awareness and empowerment in prison ministry? The following childhood recollection contains the seeds that gave rise to my passion for prison ministry and the themes that emerge in this work.

As a child of nine, because of divorce, I had been separated from my mother by thousands of miles with no contact at all. While my father was an important presence in my life at that time, he was not always an effective presence. For the most part, my day to day living was overseen by a truly "wicked stepmother." It occurs to me that the stark contrast between that time of wounded disconnection and the moment of a healing connection intertwined, may explain its immense impact on me then, and its ongoing effect to this day. For not only do I remember it clearly in my mind, I feel it deeply in my being. Indeed, the depth of feeling may be more intense now, for I can understand the experience on a far more profound level than I ever could have as a nine-year-old child.

1. Hanh, *Teachings on Love*, 48.
2. Surrey, "Relationship and Empowerment," 165.

In my two-year sojourn with this step-parent, not only was I subjected to harsh physical and emotional abuse, I was also, periodically, kept in my room for months at a time, allowed out only to go to school, or in contrast, forbidden to come home after school until my father arrived home from work. I had no choice but to walk the streets alone. Indeed, more than once, I was not allowed to live at home, and instead, I stayed with the sister of this stepmother who lived just a few blocks away. Actually, there were two sisters who lived nearby with children of their own. Together, we ranged in age from five to twelve and during the summer months we often spent our days at the beach, as the Pacific Ocean was just a few blocks away.

The summer of my ninth year was one of those times when I was not allowed to live at home with my father and stepmother and instead I lived at my step-aunt's house. Ruthie was always kind to me; she never hurt me in any way, so there was always a measure of safety I felt when I was with her family. Those summer days, we children had taken to collecting soda bottles we found on the beach and turning them in at the concession stand for nickels and dimes. Our silver added up quickly, and eagerly we bought ice cream, hot dogs, and candy bars! Soon, we felt brave and bold enough to approach couples stretched out on their beach towels, or families lunching together, to ask them for their empty bottles. By now, we were making good money!

Meanwhile, Ruthie got word of our profiteering, and one evening she gathered us together and strictly informed us we were not to approach people to ask them for their empty soda bottles. If we found them left on the beach that was fine, we could turn them in for cash, but under no circumstances were we to ask individuals for their empty soda bottles.

A few days later, on a hot August day, the six of us headed for the beach. All obeyed the new rule . . . except for me! Somehow, in my mind, I reasoned that since Ruthie was not my real mother, I was exempt from the rule. I don't even remember considering the possible consequences, but of course that evening the others informed Ruthie that I had not done as I was told. While there seemed to be no immediate repercussions, the following day as we made plans to head for the beach, Ruthie calmly told me that because I had disobeyed I would not be allowed to go with the others to the beach; I would have to stay home.

Clearly, I remember my sense of disappointment, shame, and isolation. Dejected, I found a book and took myself out into the backyard under the shade of a small tree. There I spent the morning hours reading, feeling quite alone and bereft. It was lunchtime when Ruthie appeared beside me. She had brought me a sandwich, a glass of milk, and Oreo cookies. Then, to my amazement, she sat down beside me and suggested we play a card game of rummy, one of our favorite pastimes.

In that moment, her outreach to me, her kindness, her goodness bestowed was truly a healing connection. Perhaps because it was in such contrast to the treatment I had been receiving from her sister it took on extraordinary meaning for me. To this day, Oreo cookies have a special significance for me. Indeed, I can see now that they represent the admonition given by the practicing Buddhist, Sharon Salzberg, to "cultivate the good."[3] Looking back at the experience, I fully understand her words: "When we experience mental or physical pain we often feel a sense of isolation, a disconnection from humanity and life. Our shame sets us apart in our suffering at the very time when we need most to connect."[4] The pain and rejection I had experienced at the hands of my stepmother had created a sense of isolation, shame, and disconnection. Ruthie's outreach to me at that moment helped to heal not only the isolation, shame, and disconnection I felt as a result of my disobedience, but her loving-kindness helped to heal and transform the terrible pain and suffering I was living in at that particular time of my life.

As a healing connection, it was also indeed an act of love, for as Salzberg states, "the single act of being completely present to another person is truly an act of love."[5] Moreover, it was mutually interactive and through the healing connection it also proved to be empowering as somehow it gave me back to myself. My personhood was honored, respected, and cared for. While outside that small circle of safety, I continued to experience the wrath and rejection of my stepmother, in contrast, in that moment of healing connection, I felt valuable and worthwhile. I had been responded to and affirmed, and the experience of healing connection is deeply embedded in my psyche, deeply rooted in my very being. While as a child I could never have articulated the significance of this experience, I know on a deep level the unqualified truth of those two notable psychiatrists, Jean Baker Miller and Irene Pierce Stiver, who affirm in their book, *The Healing Connection*, "we cannot develop a sense

3. Salzberg, *Lovingkindness*, 3.
4. Ibid., 9.
5. Ibid., 14.

of worth unless the people important to us convey that they recognize and acknowledge our experience."[6] We may never know the meaning a kind word or action may have in the life of another human being, yet often it can, on a certain level, mean the difference between life and death.

Undoubtedly, the truth and value of this experience deeply influences my present work in prison ministry, for the heart of that child still lives within me and the mind of this now adult woman knows unequivocally how essential it is that we are attended to and recognized. Whether we are children or adults, it is as necessary as the air we breathe. As Miller and Stiver remind us, "it must be present all through life or else we suffer terribly."[7]

Terrible suffering is what the present prison system with its motif of retributive justice incurs, for it generates isolation, shame, rejection, and loneliness; it stokes the emotional fires of anger and rage. Ultimately, it breeds deep disconnection, which only serves to fuel further cycles of violence. It is an established fact that the majority of men and women who are imprisoned have suffered severe disconnection in human relationships during their formative years, the terrible disconnection resulting from physical, sexual, and emotional abuse. Psychologist James Gilligan, who has worked in maximum-security prisons, states, "Physical violence, neglect, abandonment, rejection, sexual exploitation and violence occurred on a scale so extreme, so bizarre, and so frequent that one cannot fail to see that the men who occupy the extreme end of the continuum of violent behavior in adulthood occupied an equally extreme end of the continuum of violent child abuse earlier in life."[8]

The suffering, the pain and shame of loneliness, isolation, rejection, and abuse sow the seeds of disconnection and anger, breeding cycles of discord and violence. To one degree or another, we are all broken and wounded, and our primary purpose must necessarily be for healing and transformation of ourselves, one another, and our world. Punishment as retributive justice does little if anything to promote such healing and transformation. Restorative justice, with its foundation of shalom, of making things right, may well offer the best hope and promise.

6. Miller and Stiver, *Healing Connection*, 32.

7. Ibid., 32.

8. Gilligan, *Violence*, 45.

Towards such healing and transformation, human beings have been granted a truly awesome responsibility, the responsibility for the care and nurturing of one another, ourselves, and this world. Our lives do not need to be oppressive, miserable, or desolate. One need only look around at this vast, amazing universe we call home. It is breathtaking, awesome, and magnificent in its beauty and abundance. Within us we have the possibility, the potential for creating beauty and goodness, justice and mercy, care and compassion. All that we need has been given to us by a good and gracious God, the Spirit of Life. We need only search with all our minds, with all our hearts, with all our souls to grow in love of God, of self, and of neighbor. This is the message of the man from Nazareth, not only for Christians, but for all people everywhere, and this is our greatest challenge, our greatest task. While in the face of all the suffering and injustice in our world the task may well seem insurmountable, we need only remember that the task ahead of us is never greater than the power behind us for " if you have faith as small as a mustard seed. . . . Nothing will be impossible for you" (Matt 17:20).

Acknowledgments

FIRST AND FOREMOST, I wish to acknowledge with deep gratitude Brita Gill-Austern. Throughout this project, her wise understanding and expertise guided me, her hope upheld me, and her faith sustained me. Her encouraging words, "Snail by snail is just fine, keep moving, a page a day, every few days, a week, adds up in the end. I'm rooting for you," enabled me to keep moving along. Towards the end, as I sought out a place of silence and solitude to complete the writing, she cheered me on, "The finish line here you come!!!" Without her presence, this work would not have come to fruition.

To Sharon Thornton, I offer praise and gratitude, not only for her gentle and thoughtful manner of questioning, but most important for her journeying with me in visitation to our inmate in the College Behind Bars program. Her loyalty and companionship have been invaluable. For her special creativity and insight towards the title of this book, I am most grateful.

Thank you to Laura Tuach, a very special human being, who has been blessed with deep wisdom and was so very helpful as I tried to formulate the questions for reflection and discussion.

Much gratitude to my dear friend Marlene Gibbs who earnestly and patiently helped me to bring the Partakers College Behind Bars program to Twelfth Baptist Church in Roxbury. This could not have happened without her first-rate assistance and support.

For someone not highly skilled in the workings of the computer such as myself, my friend and neighbor, Janet Fillion has given enthusiastically and energetically of her skills and time. Her generosity and patience have been remarkable.

I also wish to thank my friend Charles Phillip Smith, who from start to finish has been a faithful presence—faithful in the sense of being full of faith in me as I moved towards the completion of this work.

Most beloved to me are my daughters, Bonnie Lyn Hemenway and Kory Donnell Hemenway, each of whom have been supportive in their own special way. For the many times I called Bonnie at work desperately needing her to rescue me from a computer obstacle, I give thanks for her knowledge and patience. Her keen insight gave shape and form to the title of this book. For Kory's sensitivity at a critical time of pressure and despondency, sending flowers with a note, "Hang in there, Mom," I give deep thanks. For their care and presence throughout this time, their gift of roses, tulips, and freesia delivered on the morning of my oral examination with the words, "Congratulations! We're very proud of you!!"—my heart overflows with deep gratitude for both of them.

Finally, even if posthumously, I must acknowledge my wise and loving mentor, Donnell Boardman, who, many years ago, saw the best in me and believed the best in me. Without his presence in my life, a presence that fostered my own healing and transformation, I would never have arrived at this place in my journey.

Deep, deep gratitude to all and to the *Spirit* that undergirds our life together here on this earth and in this universe!

Introduction

Remember those who are in prison
as though you were in prison with them.

(HEB 13:3)

THE CHALLENGE OF CROSSING OVER

THE NEW TESTAMENT ORDINANCE to remember those who are in prison is not one that is frequently prescribed in Christian churches and communities, and it is not very difficult to understand why. Prisons are not pleasant places. Prisons are not welcoming places. Prisons are those places best not seen. Indeed, in all likelihood, we would rather not even hear about prisons. Yet, at this particular time, in these early years of this twenty-first century, for many reasons, it is vitally important that we both take a look at prisons and hear about prisons because the very soul of our nation is at stake. The United States prison system is, as author Daniel Lazare states, "America's homegrown gulag archipelago, a vast network of jails, prisons, and 'supermax' tombs for the living dead that, without anyone quite noticing, has metastasized into the largest detention system in the advanced industrial world."[1]

Did you know that the United States now has the largest number of imprisoned men and women in the industrialized world? Did you know that the greatest numbers of those imprisoned are those who are poor? Did you know that the number of African Americans imprisoned far exceeds their ratio in the population at large? Did you know that the fastest growing segment of the prison population is women?[2] Lazare provides the grim fact that the United States, "with 2.2 million people behind

1. Lazare, "Stars and Bars," 29.
2. Ibid., 29.

bars and another 5 million on probation or parole, . . . has approximately 3.2 percent of the adult population under some form of criminal-justice supervision, which is to say one person in thirty-two."[3] Significant too, is that the majority of these individuals are imprisoned for nonviolent, often drug-related offenses.

However, we need not feel deficient if we are lacking in such awareness, for in the race and the rush of our modern lifestyle, most of us are just barely managing to hold our own lives and the lives of our families together. No doubt, it was the same for those ordinary folks with whom Jesus of Nazareth walked and talked two thousand years ago. To be sure, they were struggling in a different time and a different place and with different concerns, but they were still, like most of us, struggling to survive. Yet Jesus had a message, a powerful message, and it fostered awareness and empowered the people.

In our own time, it was Martin Luther King Jr. who "maintained that the social mission of the Christian Church requires that it have as its primary goal the development of the beloved community."[4] The creation of this beloved community was the bedrock of Jesus' ministry. The life and ministry of Jesus of Nazareth was all about justice and mercy; it was all about compassion and healing; it was all about shalom, making things right. The Spirit that fueled his passion to create the kingdom of God on earth is the Spirit that gave birth to the earliest Christian communities, and it is the same Spirit that lives and breathes among us today which can empower us, here and now, to build the beloved community here on earth. To build this community, we must be willing to see the dark and desolate places around us and in our midst, and we must be willing to hear the terrible truths of our own human failings. In their book, *Compassion: A Reflection on the Christian Life*, authors McNeill, Morrison, and Nouwen acknowledge, "We do not aspire to suffer with others. On the contrary, we develop methods and techniques that allow us to stay away from pain."[5] Yet Jesus calls us to compassion and "it is a call that goes right against the grain; that turns us completely around and requires a total conversion of heart and mind."[6]

3. Ibid., 29.

4. Ansbro, *Martin Luther King Jr.*, 187.

5. McNeill et al., *Compassion*, 6.

6. Ibid., 8.

Opening one's mind and heart to the realities of our retributive justice system cannot but help create a conversion, for it becomes impossible not to see the truths that live there, the truths of injustice and structural violence. These were the very truths that sparked the passion of Jesus. The injustice and oppression rooted in issues of race, class, and gender contain that source of evil understood as radical disconnection, and it is this evil that circumscribes all the suffering that our world holds. Jesus knew, unequivocally, that God's kingdom could not come on earth as it is in heaven until such evil, lodged in the structures and institutions of human society, was addressed and exorcised. God's kingdom, the beloved community, will not simply or suddenly appear among us. No, instead, we must actively participate in helping to create that kingdom here on earth. It is not up to God alone. God needs our help. Indeed, it is up to us working with God, and if we ever hope to live out our short lives in the midst of that beloved community, we must find the courage to look honestly and directly at ourselves, at those values we profess to believe in, and at our actual practice of those values. We must also find the courage to look honestly and directly at our society, at those values it professes to believe in, and the actual practice of those values. In her book *To Work and to Love*, Dorothee Soelle affirms, "We must work toward the time when the inner contradictions of a system of social injustice become so obvious that they move people from apathy to struggle, from despair to hope."[7] Then finally, we must have the courage to speak truth to power as Jesus of Nazareth most certainly did. We cannot, however, do this alone. Rather, we must do it together.

Together too, we must honestly consider our place in society. Are we privileged, are we white, are we male? Or are we underprivileged, black, Indian, Latino, female? Or, might our place in society be any of these combinations? These questions go to the heart of prison ministry, for it is not merely the prisoner one must consider; one must also consider the victim and the larger community as well. With regard to crime, author David Cayley notes in his book, *The Expanding Prison*, "it usually begins in circumstances of poverty, joblessness, family breakdown, sexual violence, drug addiction and neighborhood abandonment."[8]

Indeed, with respect to crime, whether one considers the prisoner, the victim, or the community, all are intricately interwoven and inter-

7. Soelle and Cloyes, *To Work and to Love*, 161.

8. Cayley, *Expanding Prison*, 357.

related. Jesus said, "I was in prison and you did not visit me for as you have not done it to the least of these, you have not done it to me" (Matt 25:43–45). It would seem here that Jesus was preaching a theology of mutual relation, that sort of God-talk that reminds us that yes, we are most certainly our sisters' and brothers' keepers. Visiting our sisters and brothers in prison means not only crossing over those prison walls but crossing over all those other walls that separate us out from one another, the walls of class, race, and gender, for it is only then that we can truly come to know and understand one another, and *that* understanding is called love. Yet, this crossing over we must also do together, for it is together that we can find the necessary courage to transcend our fears and come to know and feel, as author Annie Dillard describes it, "our complex and inextricable caring for each other, and for our life together here."[9]

MY OWN EXPERIENCE OF CROSSING OVER

Boundary crossings, crossing over those lines that separate us from one another, whether they be visible or invisible, has been part of my own experience and ministry for several years now. Over eighteen years ago, I began working as a visiting nurse in the inner city, the "ghetto" streets of Boston. It was a world foreign to me, having grown up in an affluent white suburb and having had essentially no close interactions with people of color. Indeed, as a child I can vividly remember two negative experiences with regard to African Americans. First, I remember as a child about the age of six, being on the beach at a lake with my mother. That day, there were only a few people there, but as my mother and I were swimming, suddenly I saw my mother racing out of the water toward our blanket on the shore, yelling at a man to come back with her wallet, which he had stolen. I saw that the man running off into the woods was black. Then, on another occasion, I remember riding on a bus with my mother one wintry evening. We had been sitting near the back of the bus and the bus had nearly emptied. A black man had come onto the bus and sat in the last seat not too far behind us. He was singing and began talking to my mother in a way that even at that young age I knew to be inappropriate, and I knew too that he had been drinking. My mother took me by the hand, and we moved to the front of the bus. In remembering those two experiences I can still feel the fear that they

---

9. Dillard, *Teaching a Stone*, 94–95, quoted in Palmer, *Let Your Life Speak*, 80.

engendered, and unfortunately the experiences involved people of color. Equally relevant, however, is my childhood experience of being given a black baby doll that I could wash and dress, and whose hair I could comb. I still remember clearly her blue cotton dress with small pink flowers, and I loved her dearly.

Then, at the age of forty-one, I returned to college to complete my undergraduate degree in nursing with a co-concentration in women's studies. The first course I took was titled, "Black Women in America," and it opened my mind and heart to an entirely new understanding of black culture and experience. The year following my return to college, I had left a comfortable, secure, secluded position as a staff nurse in a large HMO practice in the suburbs to work in a nurses' clinic of an inner-city homeless shelter. There, for the first time I came in direct contact with black folks, not just face to face, but face to feet, as one of the basic foundations of the clinic was to provide evening foot soaks to these homeless men, who had trod the streets all day in the sweltering heat of summer or the frigid cold of winter, and returned at night to the cover of the shelter for a meal and a bed, almost always intoxicated from either alcohol or drugs. While there were risks involved with working in such a setting and while it was painful and discomfiting, still there was a measure of security behind the walls and doors of the nurses' clinic, protected as it was from the larger, open areas of the shelter where the "guests" congregated, ate, and slept. A year later, when as a visiting nurse I stepped out onto the streets of the ghetto, walked through the housing projects, and into the homes of impoverished people of color, I entered an entirely new arena of experience of race, class, and poverty, and aside from the taxicab used to shuttle us from patient visit to patient visit, there was no real enclosure to facilitate a sense of safety.

Indeed, the two housing projects that were part of my day-to-day existence as I earned my livelihood as a visiting nurse were considered to be the most dangerous and dilapidated public housing in the city of Boston. Each day as I pulled open those ugly, red, heavy steel doors and stepped into the hallways, I felt the pain of such an existence. As I entered those hallways, deep in my heart of hearts there was always a prayer, as so often the stench of urine, filthy floors, and remnants of trash and garbage greeted me. Beyond the hallways, behind the individual apartment doors, there might not be too much difference between the outside hallways and the inside apartment, although occasionally one would enter an apartment tastefully decorated and immaculately clean. Yet, behind every apartment door there were people, and as I came to know the people, I grew to love both the people and the place. There was no pretense here. People were down-to-earth, genuine, humble, humorous, and warm, kind-hearted, generous and gracious, deeply appreciative and deeply spiritual. As bell hooks states in her book, *Where We Stand: Class Matters*, "To love the poor among us, to acknowledge their essential goodness and humanity is a mighty challenge to class hierarchy."[10]

Indeed, I came to know the truth of a local minister's words, "there is gold in this ghetto," and I also came to know the truth of the forces that obstructed the mining of such gold. Only a few months after I began my work here, I was completing a visit to a patient one day when I heard the cab's horn outside. Saying goodbye to my patient, I started down the inside hallway stairs. There, on one side of the landing, were two men who from all appearances were in the middle of a drug deal. Uneasily, they glanced at me, and while I felt some degree of apprehension, I knew I needed to proceed in a matter-of-fact manner. As I excused myself, I walked between them down the stairs, and out the door. Getting into the cab, I related my encounter to the other nurse with whom I shared the cab. She, being a seasoned veteran of the projects, pointed to a four-year-old boy outside the door, noting that he was their runner. I was shocked, and my naïveté shattered as my first lesson in the harsh reality of life in the ghetto sunk in.

In his book, *Losing Moses on the Freeway*, author Chris Hedges describes his own experience living in Roxbury as a young seminarian, perhaps twenty years before I arrived there. His experience was of a different time, a time not too long after the white flight from this section of the city, but before the rebuilding of sections of Roxbury that were gutted by fire in the racial unrest of the sixties and seventies, and long before the gentrification of the South End only a mile away. Yet despite the intervening years, the years between his time and my time, I came to know the truth of his words as he described his encounters with some of the youth in this neighborhood: "The world around them conspired to destroy them. The noise, the overcrowding, the poverty, the abuse, the indifference of the courts and schools, and the overburdened probation officers doomed them."[11]

10. hooks, *Where We Stand*, 164.
11. Hedges, *Losing Moses on the Freeway*, 34.

Clearly, this was my own sense as I remembered visiting a patient in the projects who had suffered a gunshot wound to his leg and was a known drug dealer. We visited him twice a day to do the necessary dressing changes to his wound. While he was not my regular patient, I was asked to see him one morning when his own nurse was unavailable. Having heard numerous stories of how difficult he could be with the nurses, I had some degree of apprehension as I entered his apartment, which was unkempt and disorderly. In such situations, I always try to enter in the spirit of the founder of the Religious Society of Friends (Quakers), George Fox, who advised us to walk cheerfully over the earth, answering to that of God in every person. While I proceeded to tend to his leg wound in a matter-of-fact manner, he began to engage me in conversation. To my surprise, I encountered no difficulty with him. He introduced me to a young woman who had opened the door; she was his significant other, and next to his bed in a bassinette was their small infant son, a beautiful child sleeping peacefully. In that moment my heart grieved, because similar to Chris Hedges's words was my own thought that given the environment into which this child had been born, the odds were already against this new human being.

A DEEPENING EXPERIENCE OF CROSSING OVER

Within a few years I had come to deeply love the people and the place where I found myself. An inner desire emerged to move there, from the affluent white suburb in which I lived, to the poor, black/Latino, inner-city ghetto. I knew full well that it was not the nursing that held interest for me. What drew me more and more to the people and the place of Roxbury was something much deeper, something that I found difficult, if not impossible to articulate; I only knew and sensed another dimension to my interactions with those I served. However, it was not until a few more years had passed that, as Quakers say, the way opened. Indeed, it opened in a truly most miraculous way, and I moved into Roxbury, the inner-city, the ghetto, the hood, often referred to fondly by folks who lived there as "The Bury." While on the surface such a move sounds easy, on the contrary I experienced deep heartache and sorrow as I left the home where I had raised my children, shedding bittersweet tears as I remembered all of the living that had taken place in that house. Later, shortly after arriving in my new setting, one that was so vastly different than the one I had left, I wept again. For although it had indeed seemed to me that God's hand was in all of this, the answers to why I had been brought to this place and what it was that I was supposed to do now that I was here were beyond all my knowing.

In his book, *The Biblical Vision of Sabbath Economics*, Ched Myers states, "People of privilege should socially relocate to live and work in proximity to disenfranchised people not primarily in order to 'help,' as in the old missionary model, but in order to view the world *from that space*."[12] While my living and working in a community of disenfranchised people had not come from any sense of *should* but rather from my heart, nevertheless, more so now than before, I was certainly viewing the world from that space.

A few weeks after moving to Roxbury, I began to look for a worship community. As a Quaker, it seemed that I *should* attend a local meeting for worship, and I did visit Beacon Hill Friends meeting one Sunday. Yet something within me felt a need, a yearning perhaps, for something more, and part of that more was to worship in the community in which I now lived and worked. In that mind and spirit I attended an African American Episcopal church, an African American Catholic church, and then an African American Lutheran church. However, only a short time prior to my actual move I had been quite serendipitously invited to attend Twelfth Baptist Church in Roxbury. I had been told it was the home church of Martin Luther King Jr. while he was studying at Boston University, and it was just a mile over the hill from my house. Now I returned there and decided that here I would worship.

Certainly, worship at Twelfth Baptist Church was unlike Quaker Meeting for worship. With the clapping, the singing, the praising of the Lord, and the Amens, it could not have been more different. Yet there was something deeper here, something deeper that I was seeking, and something deeper that was present in this church community, and that something was the Spirit, very much alive and palpable. It has been over twelve years since I began attending Twelfth Baptist Church, and in the Spirit of this worship community I have learned much about faith, humility, joy, praise, prayer, and gratitude. While the theological framework is in so many ways the opposite of my own, worshipping here keeps me connected in a spiritual way to the community in which I live and to the people whom I serve. For as Myers affirms, "The longer we are rooted in such neighborhoods, the more the issues so familiar to the poor become

---

12. Myers, *Biblical Vision of Sabbath Economics*, 61.

our own. Our work then moves from 'aid' to 'alliance,' from sympathy to solidarity."[13]

Indeed, through living, working, and worshipping in such a neighborhood, issues familiar to those that lived there certainly became familiar to me, and one of those issues was that of imprisonment. Often, in my conversations with my patients there would be mention of a family member in prison—a husband, a father, a mother, a grandson. This was brought home to me vividly during the time when I was completing an internship for a master's degree in pastoral ministry, and my placement site was none other than Twelfth Baptist Church and its prison ministry. In my work there, I met some of the very families for whom I provided nursing care in their homes. The connection between race, class, poverty, and imprisonment took on real meaning for me. This was the beginning, and as I moved later into the prison itself to offer a weekly workshop on anger, to assist with an ongoing art and spirituality class, and to support prisoners as they sought to complete their college degrees, I grew in my awareness, my alliance, and my solidarity.

Perhaps my greatest solidarity has been in relationship with one particular prisoner, a young woman whom I have been accompanying now for over four years as she makes excellent progress towards completing her college education through the Boston University / Partakers College Behind Bars program. For just as a child of nine I experienced the grace of staying in relationship, so too, have I watched this woman grow and learn, blossoming into the fullness of her humanity even amidst the oppressive prison environment she lives in day to day, week to week, year after year. I have come to know unequivocally the primary importance of mutual relationship, the urgent necessity of our caring presence, one for another. For there is no doubt, as the psychiatrist James Gilligan testifies in his work with prisoners, "the soul needs love as vitally and urgently as the lungs need oxygen; without it the soul dies just as the body does without oxygen."[14]

Still, despite alliance and solidarity, the fact remains that as a white person, even as a white woman, I remain a woman of privilege, for I have a good education, a profession with a decent salary, and a home of simplicity and beauty. However, a few years ago I had the opportunity to take part in an experiential game of privilege and this provided me

13. Ibid.
14. Gilligan, *Violence*, 51.

with some deepening awareness. In a group of fifteen men and women with one person being a young African American woman, as we stepped forward or backward in answer to the questions asked with regard to privilege and prejudice, opportunities and limitations, I discovered that I was only a short distance ahead of the African American woman who was, not surprisingly, at the bottom rung of the ladder so to speak. While I had always felt my heart to be in solidarity with those I served, this visual, more tangible insight of the forces that placed me in solidarity with those I serve helped me to better understand that the injustice and suffering I had experienced in my own life may well be what helps me to bridge those boundaries of race and class. Author bell hooks underscores this discovery for me, stating, "When I left the segregated world of my poor and working-class home environment to attend privileged-class schools, I found I often had more in common with white students who shared a similar class background than with privileged class black students who had no experience of what it might mean to lack the funds to do anything they wanted to do."[15]

Surely, in my own sphere as I live and work in the inner city, simultaneously moving back and forth between that world and the suburban world of affluence and opportunity, as I move back and forth between the inside and the outside of the prison walls, I am keenly aware of the divisions fostered through poverty, race, and class and how those divisions continually undermine the creation of God's kingdom here on earth and undermine our building of the beloved community. While initially I felt more focused on the prisoner and the immensity of the failings of the present retributive justice system, as I continued on in my ministry I came to appreciate the complexities of such a system, and how these are so deeply intertwined with our society itself. Through James Gilligan's studies on violence, I came to understand that we are all victims, victims of the terrible systemic violence embedded in the social and economic structures of our society. It matters not whether we are prisoner, victim, or the community at large because we are all in this together, and the suffering engendered as a result of such violence threatens us all.

At the same time, it is important to make very clear the fact that there are indeed individuals who pose a danger to others and these individuals must be kept apart from society. Gilligan concurs when he says, "I have no doubt that we must restrain violent people from injur-

15. hooks, *Where We Stand*, 119.

ing anyone, as long as they will not or cannot restrain themselves. That does require restricting their freedom for as long as they are dangerous. But punishment per se—the gratuitous infliction of pain or deprivation above and beyond whatever is unavoidably inherent in the act of restraining the violent—does not prevent or inhibit further violence, it only stimulates it."[16]

It would seem that if the church is to truly live out its Christian testimony as practiced by that person whom they profess to follow, Jesus of Nazareth, then it is incumbent upon Christians to exercise punishment with care and compassion, in a spirit of restoration rather than one of retribution. The relatively recent practice of restorative justice provides a new paradigm for the people of God to consider in their response to behavior deemed to be *criminal*. As Howard Zehr states in his book, *Changing Lenses*, "Whether the thrust of the Bible is on retribution or restoration is not a marginal issue. The question is at the heart of our understandings about the nature of God and about the nature of God's actions in history. It is not an issue which Christians can avoid."[17]

AN INVITATION TO CROSS OVER INTO AWARENESS AND EMPOWERMENT

The purpose of the work that follows is to provide a guidebook for congregational prison ministries, which will foster awareness and empowerment in prison ministries. Many individuals and congregations lack knowledge of the historical development of imprisonment as punishment. Chapter 1 provides a brief, concise, historical perspective of the prison system as a means of punishment. While the present retributive prison system and its growth seems an acceptable aspect of modern (postmodern) life, it has now reached crisis proportions, and there is an urgent need for an in-depth understanding of its history and its present ramifications. It is my belief that in order to be most effective in prison ministry work, we must have a better understanding of how we have arrived at this place with regard to our human understanding and treatment of wrongdoing.

Without a clear understanding of where we have been in this part of our human journey and how we have arrived, it is very difficult to

16. Gilligan, *Violence*, 150.
17. Zehr, *Changing Lenses*, 157.

move forward towards creating a new model of responding to criminal behavior. Chapter 2 will consider the relatively recent but growing practice known as restorative justice, recognizing that the roots of such practice date far back into the most primitive of human societies, as well as being found within both the Hebrew Scriptures and the New Testament. Restorative justice, with its foundational principle of shalom, of making things right for all involved, may well offer the best hope and promise for addressing human transgression and transforming our present retributive system of justice.

Against the framework of both retributive justice and restorative justice, Chapter 3 examines theological understandings of punishment in the Judeo-Christian tradition, followed by an exploration of Carter Heyward's relational theology in the context of the present retributive justice system of imprisonment. This chapter will assist congregations in understanding the present prison system as a structural system of domination, which perpetuates disconnection, and will show how disconnection breeds violence and evil. A brief consideration of Martin Luther King's theology of agape love along with Carter Heyward's understanding of evil as radical disconnection provides a framework for a vision for healing connections and restoring right relationship when we have violated our human relationships and communities.

Chapter 4 offers three vignettes towards the exploration of forgiveness in the context of both retributive and restorative justice. This chapter helps to demonstrate that in the context of retributive justice there is little if any opportunity for the healing that comes through forgiveness, whereas with the practices of restorative justice, as it brings together the offender, the victim, and the community, the humanity of all is honored, which is of primary value in facilitating genuine understanding and forgiveness.

With the understanding of the prison system as a structural system of domination perpetuating disconnection, chapter 5 will introduce compassionate witnessing in prison ministry as a way to develop awareness. I will utilize Kaethe Weingarten's model of witnessing positions: empowered/disempowered, aware/unaware. This model provides a way to develop empowered/aware compassionate witnessing, the kind of witnessing that promotes healing and connection across all boundaries of relationships and roles.

Finally, chapter 6 will explore three models of prison ministry, reflecting my own work and ministry with each. These are the Boston University / Partakers College Behind Bars program, the in-prison Alternatives to Violence Program (AVP), and the Committee of Friends and Relatives of Prisoners (CFROP). Each of these will help congregations to understand and indirectly experience ways in which they may provide prison ministry in active and meaningful ways.

In the past few decades, there has been a growing movement towards restorative justice practices in other countries as well as in the United States. Such practices inevitably necessitate a serious questioning of our present system of retributive justice, a system that serves only to promote a vicious cycle of crime and violence, offering little if any possibility for healing and transformation. The movement toward restorative justice practices in the church "have been emerging signs of hope calling for a radical reengagement of the Christian faith in criminal justice issues from a restorative justice perspective."[18] Following each chapter are questions for reflection and discussion, which will allow for congregations to radically reengage themselves in criminal justice issues. Remembering that even in the very worst offender, buried somewhere within that person is the *imago Dei*, this book is an invitation to individuals and congregations to grow in awareness and empowerment as they seek to engage in prison ministry in the context of their professed Christian faith.

18. Allard and Northey, "Christianity," 135.

1

Why Punishment?

If we hope to work our way toward a more effective approach to crime and violence, it is incumbent upon us to look at where we've been and to explore where we might go from here.

—Marc Mauer, *The Race to Incarcerate*

If we are to grow in awareness and empowerment in our congregational prison ministries, it is, indeed, incumbent upon us to consider where we have been, where we seem to be headed, and where we would hope to go. If we hope to minister effectively with knowledge and strength, we ourselves must be ready to be transformed in order that we, as compassionate witnesses, may transform the world. Jesus of Nazareth was unequivocally a compassionate witness; his ministry was rooted in care and compassion, forgiveness and mercy, healing and restoration. Since it is true that redemption lies in remembering, it is indeed incumbent upon us that we take the time to *remember*, to look back to the historical roots of punishment and imprisonment.

PUNISHMENT AS RETRIBUTION

Punishment as a mechanism for inflicting pain in retribution for an offense committed has a long history. Whether one considers that history in secular or religious contexts, punishment as retribution seems to be just a part of the human condition. There are, of course, different nuances in the term *punishment*. While the general understanding of the word implies a certain severity of penalizing for a transgression, other understandings of the word, such as correction or disciplining, hold different implications, such as bringing about improvement or educating. Indeed, at times there has been varying emphasis on aspects of improvement or educating, yet in considering the history of imprisonment as punishment, the punitive, retributive stance has been the driving motivation.

The prison as institution, as place for punishment for crimes committed, is simply a conventional and customary supposition in these early years of this new millennium. In their introduction to *The Oxford History of the Prison*, editors Norval Morris and David J. Rothman state, "it is tempting to think of them as permanent and fixed features of Western societies. Meting out punishment by a calculus of time to be served seems so commonsensical today, that it becomes difficult to conceive of a moment when prisons were not at the core of criminal justice."[1] However, when viewed over centuries of human evolution, the prison as it exists in the postmodern world is a relatively new invention as mode of punishment.

RETALIATION: THE PSYCHO-NEUROLOGICAL FOUNDATION

Punishment as retribution may be as old as the human race, for its seeds are embedded in the psycho-neurological circuitry of our brains, wired as we are for protecting our self, offspring, or territory. While punishment can indeed provide a means of correction, a means of education, such an approach requires a much more rational way of responding to a wrong committed. Instead, more often than not, it is our emotional way of responding to a wrong committed that is intertwined with our desire or need to punish retributively. The common, universal emotions of fear, anger, hurt, and rage are located not in the rational, thinking part of our brains, the neocortex, but rather in the amygdala, a small cluster of nerve pathways from which arises all emotion and passion. In his book, *Emotional Intelligence*, author Daniel Goleman notes the amygdala to be "like a psychological sentinel, challenging every situation, every perception, with but one kind of question in mind, the most primitive: 'Is this something I hate? That hurts me? Something I fear?' If so . . . the amygdala reacts instantaneously, like a neural tripwire, telegraphing a message of crisis to all parts of the brain."[2] Our tendency toward retribu-

---

1. Morris and Rothman, "Introduction," vii.
2. Goleman, *Emotional Intelligence*, 16.

tive punishment may well be linked, then, to this small almond-shaped organ nestled in the innermost recesses of our brain. It may well be linked to "the desire for vengeance which all of us are capable of feeling when we believe we are seriously wronged. It seems almost a universal human impulse."[3]

Probably, each one of us, to a larger or lesser degree, knows the experience of being hurt or threatened and the natural, immediate urge to strike back. It is, however, only through centuries of evolving civilization that personal retaliation and revenge have been channeled into more socially acceptable avenues of release. Dr. Karl Menninger states, "Personal revenge we have renounced, but official legalized revenge we can still enjoy. Once someone has been labeled an offender and proved guilty of an offense he is fair game, and our feelings come out in the form of a conviction that a hurt to society should be 'repaid.'"[4]

Such an explanation may aid in understanding the source of ancient modes of punishment through mutilation, disemboweling, and dismemberment. While these ways of punishing seem uncivilized and barbaric to our present day way of thinking, it was really not so long ago that such practices were standard means of inflicting punishment. As late as the mid-eighteenth century, in early modern Europe, brutal and savage means of punishment were inflicted on human beings. In his book, *Discipline and Punish: The Birth of the Prison*, Michel Foucault describes the punishment of a fellow charged with murder in France in the year 1757. Publicly displayed, half-naked, transported from the church through the streets to the scaffold, his flesh was torn from his limbs, while a mixture of boiling sulphur, oil, wax, and lead was poured onto his open wounds, culminating in his body being drawn and quartered by horses and his remains burnt up in a fiery blaze.[5] Such public demonstrations of punishment, while partially intended to reinforce a sense of righteousness on the part of the government and instill a sense of repentance on the part of the offender, primarily "bolstered the power of monarchs and magistrates and made it concretely visible."[6] Reinforcement of this kind of power must necessarily raise the question, For whom is the punishment, and whose interests does it serve?

3. Consedine, "Restorative Justice: Healing the Effects of Crime," 37.
4. Menninger, *Crime of Punishment*, 190.
5. Foucault, *Discipline and Punish*, 3.
6. Spierenburg, "Body and the State," 55.

PUNISHMENT IN ANCIENT SOCIETIES

The juxtaposition of state power and punishment had not always been primary. While punishment of those who had transgressed had always been a component of ancient societies, the understanding and the purpose of punishment has differed. Such differences are found during the years of the Middle Kingdom, 2050–1786 BC, in the civilizations of Egypt and Mesopotamia. In Egypt, there was an acknowledgement of a higher, sacred order, which was dependent on the right balance of creation. Here, "every injury inflicted on (or by) an Egyptian troubled the sacred order, which the pharaohs were bound to re-establish through their judiciary, legal procedures, and punishment."[7] Within the area of Mesopotamia, there arose the Code of Hammurabi, the talionic law, an eye for an eye and a tooth for a tooth. Although the more common understanding of the law is that it allowed for revenge and retaliation for wrongs inflicted, its actual purpose was to *limit* the revenge to an amount equal to the harm inflicted. States Menninger, "Hammurabi apparently instituted the law to control practices of family and tribal revenge that went further than the offenses being repaid and which were perpetuated in feuds."[8] While Hammurabi's Code is one that is familiar and often alluded to with regard to punishment, a less well-known code of punishment that was implemented a good three hundred years before the rule of Hammurabi is the Law of Ur-Nammu by King Ur-Nammu of Sumeria. This code was much less harsh and more humane in its practice, for "the crowning, dramatic feature of Ur-Nammu's law code was the elimination of vengeance from criminal procedures. Restitution and monetary fines rather than the infliction of pain were the official consequence of wrongdoing."[9]

While we may find some reassurance in knowing that in the earliest of human civilizations there *did* exist a more restorative practice towards wrongdoing, the Law of Ur-Nammu was relatively short-lived considering the centuries of human living that followed and the unquestioned tendency and propensity of human vindictiveness inherent in punishment. In fifth century BC, the Greek city-states and the Roman republic, flourishing around the same time, utilized brutal and savage forms

---

7. Peters, "Prison before the Prison," 8.
8. Menninger, *Crime of Punishment*, 192.
9. Ibid., 192.

of physical punishment, including stoning to death, dismemberment, burning, decapitation, or crucifixion. Imprisonment was common to each of them as well, though this was more often used as a place of detainment for lesser crimes until one could pay a debt owed or be brought to trial for a more serious offense. Indeed, "Greek city-states provide the earliest evidence for public punishment in the Western tradition—and for its roots in ideas of law and justice."[10] In Athens there was a group of elected magistrates known as the Eleven whose responsibility included the oversight of prisoners, the maintenance of the prisons, and announcement of executions.[11]

In a similar manner, at this time in Rome, around the fourth century BC, the first written laws were being established in the form of the Twelve Tables. These laws dealt primarily with private offenses, where the accused was brought before the magistrate and a group of citizens for a hearing and conviction. Such offenses included theft, personal injury, insult, and occasional offenses against the state. While the penalty might occasionally be payment compensation, most often the death penalty was inflicted. Simultaneously, imprisonment was utilized for debtors, which gave them a limited time to pay the debt owed or face death or exile. It is curious to note that symbolic of the power of the male head of household was the right to maintain household prisons as a means of disciplining any member of his domicile.[12]

POWER OF THE EMPEROR AND THE STATE

Beyond such exercise of household power there was the power of the emperor and the power of the state, both of which increased and expanded over the next few centuries. Courts were established, the advice of legal experts was sought, and more and more offenses were now viewed as *crimes against the state.* The unbridled power of the emperor manifested itself in harsher and more brutal punishments with perpetrators being tortured, thrown to the beasts, and crucified. Author Edward M. Peters states, "these punishments began under the early emperors and reached a peak during the third and early fourth centuries when they reached a level of ferocity that had rarely, if ever, been equaled in the ancient

10. Peters, "Prison before the Prison," 4.
11. Ibid., 6.
12. Ibid., 15.

world."[13] Meanwhile, as the city of Rome experienced unprecedented growth, increased population, and a corresponding rise in the number of private and public offenses, emperors turned to the building of more and more prisons. "By the end of the second century, if not considerably earlier, the number of prisons within the city and the Empire had increased considerably."[14] The power of the state was thereby consolidated and strengthened.

CHANGES IN PUNISHMENT WITH THE RISE OF CHRISTIANITY

Not until the fourth and fifth centuries did there begin to be a concern for prisoners and a more tempered attitude towards punishment. Such a change coincided with the conversion to Christianity of the emperor Constantine in the fourth century, and in particular with the emperors Theodosius and Justinian who were to follow him. While Constantine had legalized Christianity with the edict of Milan in 313, Theodosius had decreed in 381 that Christianity would be the only legal form of worship. In *Christianity: A Global History*, author David Chidester states, "With the advent of a Christian empire, the spiritual power of the church intersected with the political power of the Roman state."[15] As the early Christians had always fostered a spirit of loving-kindness and forgiveness to those who offended, this attitude was reflected in this intersection of spiritual and political power. Both Theodosius and Justinian set down codes relating to prisons, prisoners, and punishments "reflecting a mitigating of the most ferocious aspects of Roman criminal procedure."[16]

This merging of the spiritual and political influenced both the church and the state in the centuries following the legalization of Christianity. Bishops of the church were given judicial authority in determining punishment for those who had transgressed within their communities. Mutilation and death were not condoned, as these types of punishment would prevent the individual from seeking repentance and securing salvation. By the late twelfth century, monasteries had prisons within the confines of their grounds and as such hold a unique "contribution to the

13. Ibid., 17.
14. Ibid., 19.
15. Chidester, *Christianity*, 143.
16. Peters, "Prison before the Prison," 21.

history of prisons: the first instances of confinement for specific periods and occasionally for life for the purpose of moral correction."[17]

In particular, two popes, Boniface VIII and Innocent III, determined changes that would affect prisons and punishment procedure for centuries to come. Indeed, their influence is clearly reflected in postmodern trends of imprisonment and punishment. Boniface concluded that "imprisonment as punishment was a legitimate constituent of a universal legal system," and Innocent "revived an older method of inquisitorial procedure which had been developed in Roman imperial courts."[18] While the inquisitorial procedure was initially utilized within the confines of a church tribunal to contend with issues of heterodoxy, eventually such procedures would become the norm within the larger community, replacing the more common practice of accusatorial procedure whereby an individual who had transgressed the law would appear before a government official and members of the community. Inquisitors appointed by the pope necessarily required places to hold individuals accused while an investigation was underway. Prisons then were the locale for the accused, which ironically resulted in an increased awareness by the church of prison conditions. Consequently, early in the fourteenth century Pope Clement V sent a commission of inspectors into the prisons of southern France with resulting improvement in prison conditions.[19]

CHANGES IN PUNISHMENT WITHIN THE CHURCH AND THE STATE

While the church's oversight of prisons seemed more beneficial to prisoners, around this same time there was the increasing threat of heterodoxy, and the church moved away from its nonviolent attitudes of forbearance and mercy towards harsher punishments such as "incarceration, condemnation to wearing crosses, death by burning alive, branding, stoning, whipping, and hanging."[20] Coinciding with such a shift within the church, in the secular sphere there was the discovery of documents in northern Italy—copies of Justinian codes and laws that provided the

17. Ibid., 29.
18. Ibid., 30.
19. Ibid., 31.
20. Blomberg and Lucken, *American Penology*, 16.

foundation for the study of Roman law at the university level. The area of learned law now became such a desirable field of study, and "so prevalent was the interest in law that clerics feared the death of theology was near and that men would learn law and nothing but the law."[21] While such fears proved to be unfounded, the intense focus on the study of learned law undoubtedly led to changes in the practice of punishment with the use of written evidence and legal personnel, including judges, who now held power to decide which evidence might or might not be submitted and the degree of punishment to be imposed. Indeed, "the formal study of law gave considerable impetus to secular rulers to expand and legitimize their authority, especially their authority over wrongdoing."[22]

CHANGES IN MEDIEVAL PUNISHMENT WITH A CHANGING ECONOMY

While these changes and developments were occurring within the church and the state, by now other changes in late medieval society were taking place as well, all of which would have an impact on the evolution of the penal system. With the increased production of goods for marketing and trade, the European economy shifted from an agrarian society to a manufacturing society with a major change in its economic structure. Existing cities expanded and became more influential and new cities were created; governing powers of kings widened. Displacement of individuals from farms disrupted both families and communities; both poverty and criminal activity increased. In England, from the middle of the thirteenth century on, the number of prisons grew rapidly, and towns were mandated by the king to build jails to insure local peace and order. Punishment took on a theatrical quality as public scaffolds were built where the execution of transgressors was carried out amidst the presence of robed magistrates, clerics, and the ringing of church bells, and most towns had public gallows where the corpses of executed criminals were hung, clearly visible to all who passed by. The intent *was to instill fear and awe; to underscore both deterrence and the power of the laws and the state.* "Punishment spoke of the majesty of God and the King. It was inflicted to avenge their honor. It was offered as an example and a lesson."[23]

21. Ibid., 15.
22. Peters, "Prison before the Prison," 32.
23. McGowan, "Well-Ordered Prison," 80.

THE SHIFT FROM PUBLIC PUNISHMENT
TO PRIVATE PUNISHMENT

Yet, even as the influence of the Roman Catholic Church diminished in the wider social and cultural context and the public influence of the state flourished, by the end of the sixteenth century there was a growing tendency towards privatization, where ordinary deaths and burials were removed from the public gaze. Public executions no longer seemed to hold power to shock and awe the general populace. Instead, they became events for merriment and sympathetic alliance with the criminal. Simultaneously, within the upper class there was a growing aversion to such spectacles. Inevitably then, punishment was relegated to the private arena and the prison was the logical place. According to Peter Spierenburg, "the movement toward private punishment and the eventual triumph of imprisonment stand as the most conspicuous changes in the long-term evolution of the penal system."[24]

EXPLOITATION OF PRISONERS
AND THE TRANSFORMATION OF PRISONERS

As the system of punishment continued to evolve, variations on the theme reflected changing attitudes towards the source of criminal activity and its remedy. Bondage in the forms of the galleys, transportation, and workhouses blended punishment and exploitation of those who had transgressed the law.

With the scarcity of labor in the naval fleets of Europe, criminals sentenced to galley ships, often for life, buttressed the economy. It was not until the early nineteenth century, when slavery was declining and technology in ship building was advancing on the European continent that this type of bondage began to disappear.[25]

Transportation as a means of punishment was widely utilized by several European nations as colonization got underway. Transportation of criminals to other continents such as Australia and North America served both the demands for labor in the new territories as well as offsetting problems of increasing criminal activity and overcrowding of jails in the home country. In England alone, "some fifty thousand convicts

24. Spierenburg, "Body and the State," 61.
25. Blomberg and Lucken, *American Penology*, 18.

were transported to America between 1718 and 1776."[26] Most were young males who were often sold to smaller plantations, and not until the time of the Revolutionary War did this practice cease.

Yet a third alternative for punishment was imprisonment in a workhouse. This form of punishment took hold by the middle of the sixteenth century in England as over a hundred houses of correction, or *bridewells*, as they were termed, were built. While physical labor of those imprisoned was utilized, the purpose was not economic exploitation. Rather, "by introducing the offender to a regimen of honest labor, discipline, and moral instruction, it was believed the offender could be positively transformed. Following the transformation, the offender could then be released to society, a productive citizen."[27]

Towards the end of the seventeenth century, however, the workhouse had come to be intolerable to the people of the upper and middle classes who might be inclined to displace family members who seemed beyond disciplinary control within the family or who might bring dishonor to the family reputation. As a result, further changes in punishment and prisons evolved throughout Europe. Preferential areas were now designated for transgressors of the upper classes; "separation from the outside world rather than forced labor defined this regime."[28] Elsewhere, in the Netherlands, the *beterhuis* was established. These were private institutions where families paid for the inmates stay and profits were made by the owners. And in Germany, the solution was to build a prison in which only the worst criminals would be imprisoned. The Spinhouse, the second criminal prison, was built in Europe in 1669. This development marked a distinct change, for "without paying inmates, of course, the institution required another source of financing, which it found in the public treasury."[29] Indeed, imprisonment as punishment for criminal activity continued to expand, becoming a common form of punitive condemnation by the middle of the eighteenth century.

26. Spirenburg, "Body and the State," 76.
27. Blomberg and Lucken, *American Penology*, 19.
28. Spierenburg, "Body and the State," 72.
29. Ibid., 74.

PRISON REFORM

Between the middle of the eighteenth and nineteenth centuries in Europe, however, enormous changes took place in the organization and the appearance of the prison. The prison environment, which had once been disorderly, noisy, dirty, and foul smelling became regulated, quiet, tidy, and well kept. In the earlier years there had been an easy and informal flow of visitors, both family and friends; and when one was inside the prison walls, it was "not easy to distinguish those who belonged in prison from those who did not."[30] Gambling and drinking were activities engaged in daily by the prisoners, but after the middle of the eighteenth century it was forbidden to sell liquor in the prisons. A movement was underway to reform the prisoners and transform the prison, and by the middle of the nineteenth century, the prisoners' lives were carefully regulated, and silence as a mechanism for promoting inward conscientious reflection was of primary importance. Solitary confinement was now viewed as having moral value, as author Randall McGowan notes the praise that was given to the "ability of solitude to frustrate vice and promote virtue among prisoners."[31] Legislation was now passed appointing chaplains and surgeons to prisons with new emphasis on the care of prisoners' souls and bodies.

Reflective of the changes that were taking place in the structure and life of the prison were the changes that were taking place outside the walls of the prison during these years. With the decline of farming communities and an agrarian economy there was a steady rise in the urban population and an industrial economy that produced marked alterations in the values associated with family, work, and wealth—all transforming the very character of European society. Yet amidst such profound changes, "the only constant in the period from 1780 to 1850 was a nearly uninterrupted increase in crime and the number of prisoners,"[32] in all likelihood, a reflection of the turmoil and transformation in the larger society. Such an increase prompted a number of legislative investigations, debates, and treatises on penal policy. One book published was *The State of the Prison in England and Wales*, written in 1777 by John Howard, who had undertaken to visit prisons throughout England and

30. McGowen, "Well-Ordered Prison," 79.
31. Ibid., 85.
32. Ibid., 79.

the continent. What he found shocked him, for "the prison symbolized the antithesis of Christian charity."[33] His book had tremendous impact on the shape and form of prisons and prison life. As a result, prisoners were now mandated to wear uniforms and to receive religious instruction, and prison officials would now be paid a salary. Separate prisons were established for men and women and there was now emphasis on the style and structure of the prison edifice itself. Indeed, during this time, the English architect William Blackburn, who "designed nineteen prisons and influenced the shape of many more, expressed the ambition to use space and stone to shape human nature."[34]

INCREASING SEPARATION
FROM THE OUTSIDE WORLD

An individual perhaps most renowned during the early nineteenth century with regard to prison reform was Elizabeth Fry, a Quaker. Visiting the prisons beginning in 1813, she found the conditions appalling, and with the foundational Quaker belief that there is that of God in every person, she earnestly set about preaching to the prisoners. Her initial efforts at prison reform served as a platform from which there would be a growing involvement of Quakers in the area of prison reform. There was now greater emphasis on silence, decreased communication between prisoners, and increased use of solitary confinement. While the intent was to provide prisoners with the time and space for reflection on their misdeeds and to change their character into the person God intended them to be, the eventual outcome proved to be very different. By 1816, under Quaker leadership, the Society for the Improvement of Prison Discipline was established. While its primary purpose was to reform the offender, the resulting emphasis was on the more practical aspects of the prison itself and, "it pursued its policy through an ever more total system of policing the prison."[35] The result was increased separation from the outside world. Punishment, which for so long had been part of the public experience, was now privatized, and the prisoner behind the walls of the prison became the stranger. Such separation generated fear and anxiety among those on the outside of the prison walls towards those inside the prison, with growing

33. Ibid., 87.
34. Ibid., 91.
35. Ibid., 96.

apprehension regarding their return to the community. There was now an unmistakable stigma attached to the experience of imprisonment. States McGowan, "The average prisoner's life in 1865 was profoundly different from his life in 1780, but despite the large new prisons and the greater numbers incarcerated, the prison remained an institution strangely resistant to the intentions of its designers."[36]

PUNISHMENT IN THE NEW WORLD

Whether in Europe or in America, this phenomenon would hold true. In those early years in colonial America, there was a blending of the Old World and the New World. Punishment continued to be necessary for human transgression, but communities in the colonies were small and self-contained; neighbors monitored one another's behavior. Family, community, and the church provided the bedrock for colonial life. Seeking religious freedom, the colonists had arrived in the New World with a strict loyalty to God. Transgression was not a crime against the state but rather a sin against God. In their book, *American Penology: A History of Control*, authors Thomas G. Blomberg and Karol Lucken state, "Criminal behavior was blurred with sinful behavior; crime, sin, guilt, and punishment were understood as one."[37] Not only were theft and murder considered criminal, but also swearing, drunkenness, gossiping, and flirting were among behaviors deemed to be criminal. While the gallows were used most often for the more serious crime of murder, for those other behaviors as noted above, the most frequently inflicted punishments in colonial America were fines, whippings, the stocks, and public caging, and these were techniques of intense shaming and humiliation. While there were jails for holding individuals awaiting judgment, there were no prisons, for at this time in the infancy of this New World, there seemed to be no need. Colonial communities were small enough that the possibility of being shamed or embarrassed before one's neighbors was most often sufficient deterrence to wrongdoing. If being personally fined or publicly whipped did not deter one from criminal or sinful behavior, the gallows was simply the next and final solution.

However, by the end of the eighteenth century, and as America headed into the nineteenth century, the values and underpinnings of

36. Ibid., 80.

37. Blomberg and Lucken, *American Penology*, 26.

colonial America were shifting. The new nation, now independent from Great Britain, seeking to create its own identity, effected changes in its methods of punishment. The new nation, proud now as a new republic with democratic principles, sought to extricate itself from any semblance of a monarchial government with regard to crime and punishment. It was Benjamin Rush, a signer of the Declaration of Independence who argued successfully that only kings, who consider all those under their jurisdiction to be their property, shed their blood.[38] The new, democratic republic of America was morally superior to such a form of government. By 1820, except for the crime of first degree murder, the death sentence had been abolished. But if the criminal was not to be hanged, the question remained as to the type of punishment to be inflicted. "The answer was incarceration, to have the offender serve a term, a very long term."[39] Such a solution proved most expedient for the growing disorder in American society, a disorder created no doubt by increased population, growth of cities, changes from an agrarian to an urban economy, and the undermining of the authority of both family and church. The creation of prisons as institutions for rehabilitation and transformation of the offender offered hope and promise. "It was a heady assignment requiring imagination and innovation, and American reformers were equal to the task."[40]

THE BIRTH OF AMERICAN PRISONS

The states of New York and Pennsylvania were the first to construct prisons that would become the models for incarceration throughout the country. Both generated debate and rivalry. Both emphasized *isolation*, *regulation*, and *work*, but the difference lay in their *degree of isolation*. Prisoners in the New York facility inhabited a single cell but came together for work and meals, while those prisoners in the Pennsylvania facility spent their entire time of incarceration in solitary confinement. Common to both was the *imposition of strict and complete silence*. The eventual result of such regimentation was a growing similarity to a military model where both prisoners and guards wore uniforms, prisoners moved in perfect lockstep, and guards monitored and patrolled the prison premises. As the model took hold, "most of the facilities looked

38. Rothman, "Perfecting the Prison," 113.

39. Ibid., 114.

40. Ibid., 117.

like medieval fortresses, monumental as befit so noble an experiment. The thick walls and turrets were assurances that the prison was secure even as it promised to promote isolation and separation."[41]

Indeed, the American experiment drew some of the most famous from abroad for tours and observations of this innovative system. Yet despite its supposed advances, Alexis de Tocqueville of France and Charles Dickens of England both decried the cruelty of the system. While Dickens acknowledged the good intentions of its designers, he was convinced that they did not know what they were doing.[42] Failure of the inmates to conform to the strict order and regimentation of prison life resulted in severe corporal punishment such as being whipped, gagged with iron, or placed in a sweatbox. And yet for all the efforts towards reform and rehabilitation, as the nineteenth century drew to a close, prisons were now places of severe overcrowding and brutality. As in Europe, task forces were devised; studies were conducted; new recommendations such as probation and parole were implemented. Although prisons seemed to have no impact on crime reduction or rehabilitation of offenders, "the will to reform the institution did not cease. Simply put, Americans were not willing to part with the idea of incarceration."[43]

THE DEVELOPMENT OF THE FEDERAL PRISON

Indeed, towards the end of the nineteenth century, the federal government itself entered the prison business. While previously, individuals convicted of federal crimes were housed in state penitentiaries, with the building of the first federal prison in Leavenworth, Kentucky in 1891, another avenue for imprisonment would continue to expand. In 1902, a second federal prison was opened in Atlanta, and in 1910, the first Federal Parole Law was signed by President Taft, allowing federal prisoners the possibility for parole.[44]

By 1929, the Federal Bureau of Prisons was formed, resulting in more efficient classification and segregation of prisoners. By 1934, the Bureau of Prisons opened up a prison of last resort for those criminals who seemed to hold no possibility of rehabilitation. The infamous institution of Alcatraz was the facility to receive this distinction. Rotman

41. Ibid., 123.
42. Ibid., 124.
43. Blomberg and Lucken, *American Penology*, 61.
44. Rotman, "Failure of Reform," 167.

states, "Alcatraz inmates had virtually no privileges and little contact with the outside world."[45]

AMERICAN PRISON REFORM

Yet as Americans headed into the twentieth century, the influences of a new era, the Progressive Era, had a significant impact on the penal system. A medical or therapeutic model of rehabilitating prisoners was now deemed to be the solution. Behavioral science had taken hold and with the underlying premise that criminal behavior was the result of physical, mental, or social pathology, social workers, psychiatrists, and psychologists were now employed by the prison system. Here and there, significant though short-lived changes were visible. In New York, Thomas Mott Osborne chaired a commission in 1913 for the reform of the penal system within the state. He implemented the Mutual Welfare League whereby prisoners were given the power for self-governance and support, and when appointed as warden of Sing Sing prison, he promoted changes in dress and recreation. Attesting to the positive value of such changes, author Edgardo Rotman states, "at least for a time, Osborne achieved a prison atmosphere in which the inmates could develop a sense of responsibility by trusting each other to exercise meaningful decision-making powers."[46] However, by 1929 there was sufficient opposition to such a program by both correctional officers and politicians; both Osborne and his Mutual Welfare League were eliminated. During these same years in Massachusetts, the new Norfolk prison was established as a model reforming prison under the leadership of Howard Gill. Here again, outside pressures contributed to the demise of the undertaking as Gill was unable to limit the number of prisoners coming into the institution, with the result that severe overcrowding made it impossible to implement the positive, rehabilitative elements of his program. Most prisons had wardens who been previously employed as policemen or in the military, and their primary focus was on security, not on rehabilitation; moreover, they directed correctional officers who were for the most part unskilled and uneducated. States Rotman, "The Progressive prison was as maladaptive as its predecessors."[47]

45. Ibid., 167.
46. Rotman, "Failure of Reform," 180.
47. Ibid., 183.

MOVEMENT TOWARDS PRISONERS' RIGHTS

Such maladaptation of the prison system continued through two world wars and after, culminating in a series of prison riots in the 1950s. Prisoners were now demanding improved housing and sanitation, decent food, and medical care. The riots were not well organized, and when they subsided little if any change in prison conditions was evident. Indeed, in order to maintain control, prison officials exerted more punitive measures. It would not be until the sixties and seventies that a second wave of prison riots ensued, coinciding with the upheaval and unrest in the larger society outside of the prison in the context of the civil rights movement, the feminist movement, and the Vietnam War. Now within the prison walls inmates united across all divisions, joining together in political solidarity. In 1971, at Folsom Prison in California, prisoners engaged in the "longest, most nonviolent prison strike in history. Nearly all 2400 inmates remained in their cells for nineteen days without food, while enduring constant physical and emotional intimidation. Their demands, articulated in a thirty-one–point manifesto, called for an end to injustice and discrimination, the denial of political and legal rights to prisoners, and exploitation in work programs."[48]

Previously, in 1965, President Johnson had called for a special investigative task force, the President's Commission on Law Enforcement and Administration of Justice. This study underscored the realities of prison life, its brutality and degradation, its reinforcement of destructive, criminal behavior, and its total ineptness at preparing the individual prisoner for reentry into society. Taken together, the historical timing of events resulted in a major shift in penal reform. According to Blomberg and Lucken, "this shift in the thinking and character of punishment was reflective of a larger crisis in American society and its major institutions."[49] The emphasis was now on decentralizing the entire correctional system and providing alternatives to traditional incarceration. While the more serious criminals were still imprisoned, most offenders were diverted into community-based, work-release programs. However, these alternatives proved unsuccessful as well because for the most part such programs were not adequately funded or staffed, and like so many other human endeavors, abuses resulted. Consequently, there seemed to be no reduction in the rate of recidivism; crime continued to rise.

48. Blomberg and Lucken, *American Penology*, 140.
49. Ibid., 167.

1980, THE SWING OF THE PENDULUM:
"GET TOUGH ON CRIME"

There was growing sentiment that no type of reform was effective, and by the time of the national elections of 1980, there was an outcry for a new "get tough" approach to crime, which would have far-reaching effects on punishment and imprisonment in the United States in the next few decades.

The prison boom that erupted through the following years must necessarily be linked to political power and media influence, for while President Reagan was impressing the imaginations of Americans with the need to expand the war on drugs, in all truth, there was no real increase in the uniform crime reports.[50] Adding fuel to the fire was the 1984 Sentencing Reform Act resulting in the formulation of a table that matched specific crimes with specific punishments. While the intention here was commendable in its effort to avoid unfairness in sentencing, as in so much of all prison reform down through the ages, its effect proved to be deleterious, eliminating judicial discretion, providing prosecutors with increasing judicial and political power, and further dehumanizing the system of justice. To understand the outrageous illogic of the reform act, David Cayley offers the following example as described to him by a federal judge in Cleveland.

> He currently had a young man in front of him, he said, whose crimes were almost entirely products of misadventure rather than any viciousness in his character. Nevertheless, the judge went on, he had absolutely no choice but to sentence this young man to *fifty-four years* of imprisonment. And yet, he added plaintively, "nobody's dead."[51]

According to Cayley, during the national 1988 election, the issue of crime became even more hotly politicized. Indeed, "George Bush won that election by his relentless emphasis on a convict named Willie Horton."[52] (Horton was a Massachusetts prisoner who, while on furlough, was accused of a violent crime.) Consequently, with the heightened "get tough on crime" stance, many states resorted to old punishment tactics such as caning in Mississippi and chain gangs in Alabama, Florida, and Arizona.

50. Cayley, *Expanding Prison*, 44.
51. Ibid., 45.
52. Ibid., 46.

Additionally, changes in parole terms were adopted by many states, which further expanded the numbers of those imprisoned. Today, "fully a third of those in prison in California are there for a technical violation of parole or probation conditions."[53] When one compares this fact with the original concept of probation—which began in Boston with a shoemaker named John Augustus who visited courtrooms with the purpose of convincing judges to release delinquent boys to his care in order to find them jobs—the disjunction is a sad commentary on the evolution of punishment and imprisonment. Indeed, as noted by criminologist Jerry Miller, "Parole and probation services, which were once seen as a branch of social work whose aim was to keep people out of prison have now become ersatz police agencies whose officers wear firearms and pride themselves on how many they can get into prison."[54]

DRUGS AND PUNITIVE IMPRISONMENT

During the decades of the eighties and nineties, with justice becoming ever more harsh, the one area that would be most affected by such punitive policies was in the area of drug use. While by this time reported use of drugs had actually decreased, the new, cheaper, easily available version of cocaine, crack cocaine, was now widely accessible to the urban poor, and this population would now be targeted by the "war on drugs." With most states adopting mandatory minimum and "three strikes you're out" sentencing policies, the prison population soared. On the federal prison system alone, the impact of incarceration for use and or sale of drugs was dramatic, accounting for 74 percent of the rise in the prison population in the decade between 1985 and 1995.[55]

RACE AND CLASS

Indeed, in the last quarter of a century, the prison population has doubled and re-doubled again until the United States now has over two million people incarcerated. In his book, *Harsh Justice*, author James Q. Whitman notes, "In the year 2000, the incarcerated population reached the extraordinary level of 2 million, roughly quintupling since the mid-

---

53. Ibid., 48.
54. Ibid., 48.
55. Mauer, *Race to Incarcerate*, 34.

1970's."[56] And of key importance is the issue of race and class with blacks and Hispanics from the inner-city ghettoes of America disproportionately represented in the overall prison population. It is estimated that "one of every nine African-American males in his twenties or early thirties is now in prison or jail on any given day and one of every fourteen black children has a parent who is behind bars."[57]

It may well be that American penology practices have now become the new American apartheid practices. While to some, this may seem an exaggerated analogy, it is of critical importance to note that with disenfranchisement laws affecting those in prison as well as former prisoners, "Nationwide, one black man in seven has been disenfranchised as a consequence, while in Florida, the state with the most sweeping disenfranchisement laws, the number of those prevented from voting now exceeds 1.1 million."[58] Most are black and poor.

Race is unequivocally linked to class, and the issue of class is a key factor when considering the burgeoning numbers of individuals being sent to prison. The vast majority of prisoners come from the lower rungs of the socioeconomic ladder. Most have no high school education, and many more are illiterate with no marketable skills for employment. Author Jeffrey Reiman in *The Rich Get Richer and the Poor Get Prison*, states, "Poor people are more likely to come to the attention of the police. Furthermore, even when apprehended, the police are more likely to formally charge a poor person and release a higher-class person *for the same offence*."[59]

Perhaps an initial and natural response here is to deny or to dismiss such information as impossible, partly because it doesn't make logical sense, and partly because it threatens to dismantle our ideas and ideals about American justice and democracy. Denial of reality, however, can be horrifyingly dangerous as was the case of the Holocaust when Christians and the church buried their heads in the sand, refusing to confront the truth. The truth is, with regard to the poor and imprisonment, our class system breeds the very violence and crime we so fear. James Gilligan, in his seminal work, *Violence: Reflections on a National Epidemic*, attests, "The ruling class (all of whom are white in America) is responsible in large part, for the way in which we, as a community, have chosen to

56. Whitman, *Harsh Justice*, 3.
57. Ibid., vii.
58. Lazare, "Stars and Bars," 32.
59. Reiman, *Rich Get Richer*, 116.

distribute our collective wealth (since they, or those who represent their interests write the laws that constitute those choices), which is in turn responsible for the social inequities that lead to crime and violence."[60]

While it is an established fact that poverty is a source of crime, those individuals who *do* have the power to alter that fact, that is, providing adequate education and marketable skills training to those who are poor and uneducated, fail to do so. Indeed, Gilligan cites Senator Charles Schumer, whose words provide credence to this understanding, "it is in the political interest of the party that represents the interests of the very rich to foster as high a rate of crime as possible; and even to exaggerate what the crime rate is, to foment fear and panic about violent crime far beyond what is realistically appropriate."[61]

In this way, the class system is bolstered and reinforced. In this way, the middle class is provided with a lower class to fear and to which they may feel superior, which simultaneously allows them to be subordinated to and exploited by the upper-ruling class. By fomenting "fear and panic" the upper class distracts the middle class from any anger or resentment they might be inclined to feel towards the upper class. In *Race to Incarcerate*, Marc Mauer voices agreement: "A society's level of incarceration may be related to its political and economic structure. A society such as the United States, which contains a greater disparity of wealth than other industrialized nations, will therefore be more likely to display harsher cultural attitudes toward sentencing policy than will a nation with a broader social welfare outlook and system."[62]

Both the politicians and the media do their best to project the image of the *poor* criminal as the most violent and the one to be most feared, when indeed, "most crimes committed by the poor are against the poor themselves" as noted by Jeffrey Reiman, who states, "In 2003, households with an annual income of less than $7,500 were victims of violent crimes at a rate nearly three times that of households earning $75,000 and above. Rates of victimization by crimes in all categories are substantially higher for the poorest segment of the population, and drop dramatically as we ascend the economic ladder."[63]

60. Gilligan, *Violence*, 186.
61. Ibid., 186.
62. Mauer, *Race to Incarcerate*, 39.
63. Reiman, *Rich Get Richer*, 170.

However, as long as the image of poor criminals can be projected as posing the greatest threat to the lives and safety of Americans, the wealth and privilege of those upper-class Americans with money and power is protected. Reiman maintains that a potent ideological message is thereby conveyed: "the threat to law-abiding Middle America comes from below them on the economic ladder, not above them" and "the poor are morally defective, and thus their poverty is their own fault, not a symptom of social or economic injustice."[64]

In this way, the average middle-class American is blinded to the numerous ways they are harmed by the powerful and affluent. Reiman states,

> the very persistence with which the system functions to appre-
> hend and punish poor crooks and ignore or slap on the wrist
> equally or more dangerous individuals is testimony to the stick-
> ing power of this deception. That Americans continue to tolerate
> the comparatively gentle treatment meted out to white-collar
> criminals, corporate price-fixers, industrial polluters, and polit-
> ical-influence peddlers while voting in droves to lock up more
> poor people faster and for longer sentences indicates the degree
> to which they harbor illusions as to who most threatens them.[65]

As Gilligan also states, "It is not in the vested interest of the ruling class to pursue those social policies that would cut down on crime; on the contrary it is in their interest to keep the crime rate as high as possible."[66]

WHO BENEFITS

The benefits of locking up more people for longer periods of time increase still further. With the quadrupling of the prison population in the last twenty-five years, it goes without saying that state budgets have been more than strained. Consequently, private companies have come forward to offer "assistance." Reiman provides the sobering fact that, "in the ten years from 1985 to 1995, the number of prison beds under private management grew from 935 to 63,595, an increase of nearly 7,000 percent!"[67]

---

64. Ibid., 170.

65. Ibid., 181.

66. Gilligan, *Violence*, 186.

67. Reiman, *Rich Get Richer*, 171.

As a result, prisons and prisoners have become a lucrative market for corporations. Indeed, prisons have become big business. The "military-industrial complex" coined by former President Eisenhower back in the fifties has now shifted to the "prison-industrial complex." Indeed, Cayley offers the solemn reminder, "Forty years ago President Dwight Eisenhower warned his fellow citizens against the growing power of what he termed the military-industrial complex. Today, with the Cold War at an end, a new prison-industrial complex seems to be taking its place as the major threat to democracy and civil rule."[68]

Notwithstanding the enormous monetary benefits to the powers that be, other sectors within the American landscape have also inadvertently benefited. Considering that between "1985 and 1995 federal and state governments opened a new prison a week to cope with the flood of prisoners,"[69] locations of land were required on which to build these new prisons. Since no one wants a prison in *their* backyard, more often than not, sites for such facilities are established in impoverished rural communities, becoming a base for the economic growth of these communities.

Needless to say, more prisons require more employees, specifically correctional officers. This aspect of the prison-industrial complex further proliferates the "benefits" and monetary profits. In *The Expanding Prison*, David Cayley notes, "In August of 1996, 5000 jailers gathered in Nashville, Tennessee, for the annual convention of the American Correctional Association. Accompanying their meeting was a trade show comprising more than 600 booths . . . the conference brochure called corrections a 'Fortune 500 industry' with revenues of 26 billion (U.S.) in 1995."[70]

Consequently, the power of money and increasing numbers of individuals comprising the prison-industrial complex provide millions in campaign contributions to political candidates. The result has been, as Cayley notes, "to turn the employees of the crime control industry into a formidable lobby with a vested interest in further growth. The political influence of the lobby can be measured by a study of campaign contributions in California in 1991–1992, which found that California Correctional Peace Officers Association was the state's second-largest

---

68. Cayley, *Expanding Prison*, 44.

69. Mauer, *Race to Incarcerate*, 1.

70. Cayley, *Expanding Prison*, 43.

political donor, spending around $1 million in political contributions for the governorship and the legislature in each electoral cycle."[71]

THE SUPER-MAX PRISON: A NEW SECURITY MACHINE

Still, a more recent addition to the growing prison-industrial complex has been the super-max prison designed to be "the perfect, no-touch security machine for managing difficult people."[72] When in 1990, the super-max prison Pelican Bay in California opened, it was hailed as innovative, top-of-the-line, and a standard for the rest of the nation to follow. Here, prisoners had no face-to-face contact with the correctional officers or other prisoners. The cells were windowless and prisoners were within their cells for over twenty-two hours a day. A guard in a control booth electronically opened and closed the doors of the cell and food trays were passed through slots through the cell doors made of perforated metal. The guards communicated with the prisoners by means of a speaker system.[73]

However, just a few years later in 1993, a class action suit provided testimony to the fact that, despite all our creative capacity, our human vision and understanding is severely limited. The findings of the suit were that, "the extreme isolation the prison's design imposed was producing madness in the inmates and brutality in the guards. Prisoners had been hogtied, caged, and assaulted, their heads bashed into walls and floors while they were shackled, their bodies repeatedly kicked and hit with batons, their teeth knocked out, their jaws fractured, their limbs broken, and their bodies burned with scalding water."[74]

The ruling concluded that this super-max prison violated the Constitution. While changes were mandated, nevertheless, such facilities continued to be constructed with a new "Alcatraz of the Rockies" located in Florence, Colorado, where prisoners are "subject to the same regimen of total isolation and remote control that was tried at Pelican Bay."[75] Nils Christie, professor of criminology at Oslo University, has spoken extensively of his deep fears that such unprecedented prison ex-

71. Ibid., 54.
72. Ibid., 52.
73. Ibid., 52.
74. Ibid., 52–53.
75. Ibid., 53.

pansion may become a "cancerous growth," giving him "an unpleasant feeling of being in central Europe during the 1930's."[76]

IMPRISONMENT AND THE "WAR ON TERRORISM"

The "war on drugs" of the eighties evolved into the "war on crime" of the nineties, and now in this new millennium, almost daily, we are bombarded and besieged with the "war on terrorism." If the direction in which we seem to be moving was not so frightening, as noted by Christie, our evolving so-called wars of these last three decades might seem almost comical. However, with this new "war on terrorism," the manifold numbers of arrests, imprisonments, and detention of immigrants requires a heightened sense of awareness and serious attention.

With the destruction of the Twin Towers on September 11, 2001, the United States Immigration and Naturalization Service (INS) was reorganized under the Department of Homeland Security. While its functions continue under the general INS heading, its function in detaining immigrants has now been shifted to the Bureau of Citizenship and Immigration Services.

Since the great flux of immigrants to the United States in the eighteenth century, immigrants have been vulnerable to the criminal justice system. "In 1797, 70 percent of the prisoners in the Walnut Street Jail in Philadelphia were immigrants."[77] While at that time, imprisonment of immigrants was utilized as a means of enhancing their absorption into the mainstream culture, following World War II, the INS "developed a network of detention centers, and the focus of immigration policy shifted from imprisonment and acculturation to detentions and expulsion."[78]

The very reasons that impelled individuals to settle in the New World hundreds of years ago are still the same economic and political reasons that people today seek to settle in America. The recognition that those who currently enter the United States "are now photographed, fingerprinted, detained, or expeditiously removed if they enter without proper documents,"[79] stands in stark contrast to those first Europeans who arrived on the shores of North America without one piece of docu-

76. Ibid., 55.
77. Magnani and Wray, *Beyond Prisons*, 108.
78. Ibid., 108.
79. Chang-Muy, "Detention of Migrants," 100.

mentation and stands in contrast, as well, to the long-held symbol of American pride and freedom, the Statue of Liberty, welcoming the poor, the tired, and all those yearning to be free.

Under the jurisdiction of the Immigration and Naturalization Service (or the Bureau of Citizenship and Immigration Services), there are both migrants and refugees. To enter the United States legally, proper documents are required, and if these are lacking, the individual migrant or refugee is either detained or deported. While the Immigration and Naturalization Service operates several of its own detention centers, most detainees are held in federal or state prisons. If after an immigration hearing, an individual is determined to be an actual refugee, that person is released and may apply for citizenship after one year. For most detainees, however, the amount of time they are held may be months or years. Indeed, "some Cuban immigrants have been held in United States prisons for more than fifteen years without a criminal conviction."[80]

In addition to the detention of migrants and refugees, there is also the detention of permanent residents who are not citizens and who have been charged with a crime. These individuals must first serve their prison sentence and then, on completion, they are transferred to the custody of the Bureau of Citizenship and Immigration Services. "Then they are deported, even if the felony was minor, even if they were permanent residents before the conviction, and even if the rest of their family members are law-abiding permanent residents."[81]

Such punitive measures are in large part attributable to the constraining and coercive immigration laws of 1996 signed by former president Bill Clinton. For if one looks at INS figures prior to this time, "half of such cases would have been granted relief from deportation based on ties, such as work and family, established in this country."[82] Facing deportation holds its own complexities because for many individuals their home country has no repatriation agreement with the United States. Consequently, they face indefinite detention for months and years. "Of its total population of about 23,000, the Immigration and Naturalization Service is holding between four and five thousand such detainees who cannot be deported because their 'home' countries will not accept them."[83]

80. Magnani and Wray, *Beyond Prisons*, 110.

81. Ibid., 110.

82. Dow, "Secrecy, Power, Indefinite Detention," 93.

83. Ibid., 94.

The increase of immigrants imprisoned has compelled the INS to contract with state prisons and private prisons to house such individuals. This only serves to exacerbate the problems. Detainees are not entitled to whatever programs are available to other prisoners; they are moved to whatever facility has an open bed with no regard for the level of security, which means they may be placed with the most violent of inmates. The private prison industry poses grave risks for those caught in the net of the INS, for when the goal is profit, it follows that more is better, and in this context, more is equivalent to more and more immigrants who can be detained. "Today, the policy in the United States of detaining migrants, coupled with the various forces of economics and politics, has resulted in a prison population in which, by and large, First World keepers and guards imprison Third World people."[84]

Still more unsettling is the military and vigilante tactics with regard to securing our own borders. Amidst the recent debate in Congress concerning reform of the immigration laws, former president George W. Bush repeatedly provided the reassurance of making the border between the United States and Mexico more secure. With the Gatekeeper Program begun in 1996, barriers had already been erected. The border is increasingly militarized, with the building of a dividing wall, an increased number of guards, and an exponentially increased number of armed officers with the result that "between 1994 and the fall of 2005, approximately 3,600 people died crossing the border in California, Arizona, and Texas."[85] Even more disturbing and actually quite frightening are the recent vigilante groups of citizens who, believing the government has taken insufficient action with regard to illegal immigrants, have from time to time taken it upon themselves to round up individuals crossing the border and hold them until the border patrol is contacted.[86]

WHERE ARE WE HEADED?

Considering the harsh realities of the current American system of punishment and imprisonment compels us to ask, What kind of a people have we become, and what kind of a country do we inhabit? In *Race to Incarcerate*, Marc Mauer declares, "Our nation locks up offenders at a

84. Chang-Muy, "Detention of Migrants," 102.

85. Magnani and Wray, *Beyond Prisons*, 109.

86. Caroline Issacs (American Friends Service Committee, Arizona), in conversation with author, March 2008.

rate six to ten times that of most comparable countries."[87] Such a statistic goes against the grain of our American ideology.

Yet with harsher, punitive practices and with the ever-increasing numbers of criminal-justice employees and dollars spent, the return on such an outlay is sobering indeed. As Jeffrey Reiman states, "where we used to have the third-highest rate of incarceration in the world, behind South Africa and the (now former) Soviet Union, we have now pulled ahead of these two paragons of justice to lead the world in the percentage of inhabitants behind bars."[88] It should not be surprising then, as observed by David Cayley, "a number of worried professionals in both the academy and the criminal justice system have publicly expressed their fears that, without reform, an ever-expanding prison system will eventually incubate new forms of totalitarianism."[89]

In considering the evolution of punishment practices and imprisonment over many centuries, it may well be accurate to conclude that little if any real progress has been made. To honestly acknowledge this truth may be a first step in creating genuine transformation of our system of punishment. Authors Blomberg and Lucken, citing D. J. Boorstin's work, *The Discoverers: A History of Man's Search to Know His World and Himself*, comment, "Boorstin concludes that mankind's progress rests not so much in knowing, but quite the opposite, in recognizing how little indeed we do know."[90] It is quite possible, of course, to continue on the same path with the same tunnel vision, but given the current trends in imprisonment, the future does not bode well.

It seems quite accurate to conclude that the trajectory of retributive punishment and imprisonment has led to more and more disconnection and not at all towards healing and restoration. As L. Harold DeWolf states, "If we set out to devise a system to *de*humanize people we might as well use as ideal model an average prison."[91] The dehumanization and disconnection resulting from a retributive system of punishment only serves to exacerbate violence, as psychologist James Gilligan testifies out of his own first-hand experience working within prisons:

---

87. Mauer, *Race to Incarcerate*, 9.

88. Reiman, *Rich Get Richer*, 24.

89. Cayley, *Expanding Prison*, 348.

90. Blomberg and Lucken, *American Penology*, 224.

91. DeWolf, *Crime and Punishment in America*, 171.

Punishment does not inhibit or prevent crime and violence, it does not lower the rate or frequency of violence. Punishment stimulates violence; punishment causes it. The more punitive our society has become, the higher our rate of violence (both criminal and non-criminal) has become.[92]

If, then, we consider where we have been and the place to which we have come with regard to our system of retributive justice, it would seem only wise to pursue a different path with regard to wrongdoing and punishment, to pursue a new path, a more hopeful path that would foster healing and reconnection of all those concerned. That path of hopeful promise is the path of restorative justice.

QUESTIONS FOR REFLECTION AND DISCUSSION

1. What surprised you about the history of the American prison system? Did you know of the theological roots of punishment and how it has been systematized? What are your reactions and feelings to this information?

2. What are the values Christianity and your local church uphold that support the prison system with regard to the current understanding of crime and punishment? What values stand in contrast to the current system?

3. Read the following passages of Scripture with regard to the concepts of an eye for an eye and love of neighbor: Exod 21:24 and Matt 5:38, Lev 19:18 and Mark 12:31. How do you reconcile the tensions in these biblical narratives? As a group, reread p. 4. Explore how misinterpretation of the biblical code has perpetuated the current system of punishment.

4. What might be some reasons why the system of imprisonment has continued to be maladaptive despite good intentions and repeated efforts towards reform?

5. What steps can your faith community take to call for a change in attitudes and practice with regard to punishment and imprisonment? What are you willing to do to bring about this change?

---

92. Gilligan, *Violence,* 184.

2

An Alternative to Retributive Punishment:
The Hope of Restorative Justice

Restorative justice calls for a more healing stance from which to carry out justice. Finding that stance calls for vision and hard work. It depends on learning more about crime and the people caught up in it. It demands searching for better ways than imprisonment. It requires the painful work of learning how to live together well. It invites those who have the will, to work together in finding the ways.

—SUSAN SHARPE,
RESTORATIVE JUSTICE: A VISION FOR HEALING AND CHANGE

RESTORATIVE JUSTICE:
A PATH OF HOPE AND PROMISE

INSTEAD OF THE CORE of punishment being centered on retributive justice, one new and hopeful direction is the relatively recent movement towards restorative justice. While the principles and values of restorative justice are centuries old, rooted in the most ancient of human cultures, the current practice of restorative justice may be traced to the Mennonite faith community in Ontario, Canada. There in the 1970s, when a small group of Christians were discussing a community incident in which two young men were being held in the vandalizing of several properties, the possibility of the offenders meeting their victims and making reparations was raised as an alternative to the usual, harsh, retributive justice process. For these Mennonites, it seemed a way to put into practice their faith as well as their peace testimony. Coincidentally, one member of the group was also a probation officer and was involved in this particular case. When the time came to recommend the sentence to the judge, he offered his proposal. Initially, the judge dismissed it as unfeasible but when the actual time came for sentencing, to everyone's surprise the judge did indeed mandate that the young men encounter their victims face to face and make reparations. As a result, the Victim Offender Reconciliation Program, referred to more commonly as VORP, was initiated.[1] Since that time the restorative justice movement has grown into an international practice.

CRIME AS A VIOLATION OF HUMAN RELATIONSHIPS

Basic to restorative justice is the foundational premise that a crime committed is a violation, a rupture of relationships between persons. It is *not*, as retributive justice maintains, a violation of the state. A *real* person, the victim, has been harmed, and that harm must be made right. The state as an abstract entity cannot right the harm; only the perpetrator of the harm, the offender, can right the harm. In *Restorative Justice: A Vision for Healing and Change*, Susan Sharpe states, "Restorative justice offers a very different kind of experience, because it gives victims a role in the justice process, and it holds offenders accountable for repairing, as much as possible, the damage caused by their criminal action."[2] Restorative justice places the victim, not the state nor the offender, center stage. It considers as primary the victim's needs, and the one who has offended must respond directly to those needs in the fullest way possible. The primary purpose of restorative justice is not punitive; its primary purpose is healing.

Healing of the harm inflicted requires the offender to be held accountable *to* the victim. The offender must own the responsibility for the violation and consequently shoulder the obligation to make things right. In this way, the relationships between people are honored and the interconnections between individuals and communities are made visible. Longtime advocate of restorative justice, Howard Zehr, reminds us, "In the Hebrew Scriptures, this is embedded in the concept of shalom, the vision of living in a sense of 'all-right-ness' with each other, with the creator, and with the environment."[3]

1. Zehr, *Changing Lenses*, 158.
2. Sharpe, *Restorative Justice*, 1.
3. Zehr, *Little Book of Restorative Justice*, 19.

Within the present criminal justice system with its primary focus on retributive punishment, such a vision of shalom is nowhere on the horizon. With so narrow a focus, little if any possibility exists for healing of persons and human relationships. Yet a fact that is hardly considered is that the majority of individuals incarcerated will return to the community. In his introduction to *The Spiritual Roots of Restorative Justice*, Michael L. Hadley asks, "How do we want them to be when they return to us?" and simultaneously he notes, "The question is important for over 54.2 million people in the United States have criminal records." Again, he poses a question, "Is there a better way of doing the justice business?" and he reminds us, "Answers to these questions strike to the root of societal values."[4]

Our ways of practicing justice most certainly reflect our attitudes and values. Retributive justice with its emphasis on the infliction of punishment, imposing upon the offender the pain deserved for the crime committed, reflects a punitive and vengeful attitude. Restorative justice, however, speaks of different values, reflecting attitudes of compassion, forgiveness, and restoration. Surely, these were the values of Jesus of Nazareth, attitudes he lived and practiced towards others whether it was the tax collector, the prostitute, or the criminals hanging on the crosses beside him. It would seem that if we are to call ourselves Christians then we must ask ourselves how closely *we* live and practice such attitudes and values. As authors Pierre Allard and Wayne Northey attest, "a Christian reading of the Hebrew Scriptures, the life and ministry of Jesus, and the overall witness of the New Testament, point to what we would describe as a restorative justice model and practice in response to crime."[5]

The values and attitudes of restorative justice based upon the foundational principle of making things right for all involved, the victim, the offender, and the community, as reflected in the concept of shalom, requires a transformation of our thinking in response to wrongdoing. Rather than reacting in a spirit of retaliation, it calls for responding in a spirit of love, that same kind of love reflected in the life and ministry of Jesus, the kind of love that provides for the possibility of healing and transformation. As one victim noted, who in response to the crime perpetrated experienced restorative justice practices, "Today I have ob-

---

4. Hadley, "Introduction," 8.
5. Allard and Northey, "Christianity," 119.

served and taken part in justice administered with love."[6] If our primary purpose is for healing and transformation, it is critical to understand that the present retributive justice system, with its harsh and vengeful punitive attitudes, contributes to practices of shaming that lead to the disintegration of individuals and their relationship to self, other, and community. In contrast to such *disgrace shaming* is *discretionary shaming* or is what is referred to in restorative justice as *reintegrative shaming.*

THE REINTEGRATIVE SHAMING
OF RESTORATIVE JUSTICE

Restorative justice, with its primary focus on healing the harm that has been inflicted, stands in sharp contrast to criminal justice, with its primary focus on punishment. Indeed, within the restorative justice framework there has been a deepening understanding of the consequences of punishment as retribution. The impact of such a stance on those imprisoned is to instill a sense of shame, and what is *essential* to understand is that there are key differences in the emotion of shame.

Shame is universal; it comes with the territory of being human in this world. Shame is an affect, a feeling, an emotion, just as is the emotion of joy. Unlike joy, however, which is positive and life-giving, shame is often negative and, more often than not, it is life-diminishing whether it is momentary or enduring. "To feel shame is normal. But too little or too much shame may produce unique difficulties."[7]

Psychologists have made the distinction between discretion shame and disgrace shame. While the feeling of shame is distinctly discomforting, the imagined discomfort of discretion shame actually protects us from choices that would lead us to transgress societal rules, standards, or mores. Equally important, it serves to protect our inner selves in choosing the degree and content of exposure of ourselves to others. Disgrace shame, however, is more than discomforting; it is deeply painful, cutting into the core of our being. Theologian James Fowler states, "Shame involves a painful self-consciousness in which we feel exposed to others and to ourselves as deficient, weak, or helpless—and, at worst, contemptible."[8] The pain associated with shame, which can often be

6. Braithwaite, "Does Restorative Justice Work?" 327.

7. Lewis, *Shame*, 12.

8. Fowler, *Faithful Change*, 92.

excruciating, makes it an extremely difficult subject to contemplate. Indeed, to converse about shame stirs up the emotion of shame itself, for as the psychiatrist, James Gilligan, reminds us, "nothing is more shameful than to feel ashamed."[9] How shame is experienced and how it is processed is crucial in relation to self and in relation to others. It is also crucial that we understand this as it regards the shaming effects of retributive punishment.

The degree and intensity of experiences of shaming play a key role in one's identity and self-worth. To the extent that one has been shamed repeatedly and extensively, the core of one's being has been severely wounded. Indeed it can seem as if one's very self is in jeopardy of being annihilated. Gilligan states, "To be overwhelmed by shame and humiliation is to experience the destruction of self-esteem; and without a certain amount of self-esteem, the self collapses and the soul dies."[10] It is worth noting that in his work with prisoners, many of whom committed some of the most violent crimes, Gilligan came to know firsthand that these individuals had themselves experienced severe forms of physical, sexual, and emotional abuse. The shame they endured as a result of such abuse so threatened the annihilation of the essence of their selves, their souls, that the annihilation of another seemed to be the only means for their own survival. In this way, disgrace shaming is disintegrative shaming; it is a vicious cycle of violation of self and other, breeding violence itself. As Gilligan states, "The emotion of shame is the primary or ultimate cause of all violence, whether toward others or toward the self."[11]

That the present criminal justice system perpetuates disgrace shaming or disintegrative shaming can easily be discerned in the context of initiation into the prison system. On arrival, the individual is immediately subjected to a process that is intended to be degrading and humiliating, specifically for the male inmate. Under the assumption that a new inmate may be attempting to smuggle drugs into the prison, he is forced to strip naked in the presence of correctional officers, then to bend over and "spread the cheeks of his buttocks so that his anal orifice is completely exposed to the group. At this point, an officer sticks a gloved finger into the man's anus."[12] In much the same way that, centuries ago,

9. Gilligan, *Violence*, 111.

10. Ibid., 48.

11. Ibid., 110.

12. Ibid., 154.

the punishment of offenders in the public square was intended to shock and awe, and to demonstrate the clear and unequivocal power of the king, so too today this initiation process is intended to demonstrate the power of the prison and "to intimidate him into submitting absolutely to the institution and its officers."[13] Gilligan notes further,

> The symbolism is obvious; it is a digital anal rape. But even before the finger is introduced into the anus, it is a public humiliation. It is a total degradation ceremony, a massive assault on and annihilation of manhood. With at least some inmates it achieves— in conjunction with other components of the admission process and the total incarceration experience—the intended aim of total degradation ceremonies: ritual destruction of the personality or manhood of the inmate, the death of his self, so that he becomes a "non-person," or a "dead soul."[14]

To consider shaming, however, within the context of restorative justice, casts an entirely different light on the experience of shame. The Australian, John Braithwaite, a strong advocate of restorative justice, has written extensively on the distinction between disintegrative shaming and reintegrative shaming. Currently, our western model of punitive imprisonment fosters shame that is stigmatizing. Braithwaite attests, "stigmatization is the kind of shaming that creates outcasts; it is disrespectful, humiliating."[15] Retributive justice casts the offender as an evil person while restorative justice perceives the essential goodness of the person while acknowledging the harmful *act* as evil. While shame is an ingredient of both, there is world of difference between the two.

The first, disintegrative shaming, casts the individual out from family, friends, and the community while simultaneously fostering self-alienation. The latter, reintegrative shaming, while providing strong and clear disapproval of the offending action, allows the individual to maintain self-respect. It does so by holding the offender directly accountable to actual people, the victim and the community, then seeking ways to restore right relationships as well as receiving the offender back into their home community.

Retributive justice, claiming as it does, that the criminal action has violated *the state*, impersonal as the state is, may indeed diminish feel-

13. Ibid.
14. Ibid.
15. Braithwaite, "Restorative Justice," 85.

ings of authentic guilt on the part of the offender. While the primary aim is to determine guilt, once guilt is established and the individual banished to the prison, the ensuing isolation, alienation, and stigmatization of the offender insures a sense of shame that is debilitating to one's sense of self and one's sense of self-worth.

According to James Gilligan, there is indeed a connection between guilt and shame, but not in the way one might ordinarily consider. Harsh punishment actually increases feelings of shame and decreases empathy towards others, as well as guilt.[16] It is extremely important that somehow we come to understand this connection. For as Gilligan attests, "the more harshly we punish criminals, or children, the more violent they become; the punishment increases their feelings of shame and simultaneously decreases their capacities for feelings of love for others and of guilt toward others."[17] Out of his firsthand experience with prisons and prisoners, indeed with some of the most violent individuals, Gilligan has come to believe that, "nothing stimulates crime as powerfully and as effectively as punishment does (since punishment stimulates shame and diminishes guilt and shame stimulates violence, especially when it is not inhibited by guilt)."[18]

Retributive punishment and its consequent stigmatization are not limited to a specific court sentence of months or years. The stigmatization of disintegrative shaming is never-ending as reflected in disenfranchisement policies, housing and job discrimination, and the barring of federal loans for purposes of education. With deep and terrible shame, one carries that scarlet letter *A* branded on one's forehead for a lifetime.

RESTORATIVE JUSTICE
AS A DIFFERENT PERSPECTIVE ON CRIME

Consequently, not only does restorative justice offer a very different kind of experience, it presents a very different perspective on crime. A crime is not simply an isolated act of an isolated individual. The criminal action is a reflection of the individual's roots in family and community. While the victim and the harm suffered by the victim is held as central, there is also, at the same time, the recognition that in all likelihood the

16. Gilligan, *Violence*, 113.

17. Ibid., 113.

18. Ibid., 187.

offender too has been the victim of harm, for it is an established fact that most offenders have suffered abuse and violence in their own individual lives, which often has a direct bearing on the harm they themselves have inflicted. Living in right relationship does not simply mean that the offender be held accountable, but also that families and communities be held accountable for the causes that may have contributed to the crime. "Individuals are responsible for choices they make resulting in harm to others, but collectives at the neighborhood, city, county, state, or national level are responsible for social conditions that increase the likelihood of crime."[19]

In this way as well, restorative justice stands in stark contrast to retributive justice. In the context of our present criminal justice system, the focus and emphasis is on the individual offender. There is little, if any, consideration of the victim, and essentially no consideration of the community, including the family and the community at large, which has given birth, so to speak, to the offender. Indeed, "because factors such as racism and poverty are outside the control of individual offenders, holding offenders accountable for individual harm, without accountability for the harms of social inequities, risks reinforcing an unjust social order."[20] We fail to ask, Who comprises the offender's family? What might be their psychosocial problems and struggles? What kind of neighborhood does the offender come from? Are there issues of race and class? What are the structural inequities? Have poverty, lack of education, lack of employment and opportunity been factors in the development of the offending individual? Such questions, which probe more deeply into the complexity of human lives, which might provide for a more compassionate response to criminal behavior, are outside the sphere of retributive justice.

Restorative justice, however, almost always considers such questions. While restorative justice practices cannot solve structural inequities, its values of healing and restoration, of seeking wholeness for the community offer a different paradigm for human relationships and human living. Kay Pranis affirms this when she says, "a restorative community is a learning community, a community that learns about itself from those who have been hurt and those who have caused hurt, and uses that learning to improve community life for all."[21]

19. Pranis, "Restorative Justice, Social Justice," 288.
20. Ibid., 287.
21. Ibid., 289.

Indeed, if restorative justice remains true to its values and vision of shalom, it necessarily embodies the values of social justice whereby the physical, social, emotional, and economic well-being of *all* members of the human family are of critical concern. The systemic issues that are so often at the root of criminal behavior must be addressed if real and lasting change is to occur. In *Beyond Prisons*, authors Laura Magnani and Harmon L. Wray state, "This requires the community to accept responsibility by committing itself to implement the changes in social structures that will genuinely prevent crime at its roots."[22]

PRACTICES OF RESTORATIVE JUSTICE

Understanding the relationship between individuals, families, communities, and the larger society amidst the social, economic, and political structures that bind them together is greatly enhanced by restorative justice practices. The three practices that have evolved over the last quarter century are *victim-offender mediation, community conferencing,* and *community peacemaking circles.* "All three practices reflect the same aims: to put key decisions into the hands of those most affected by a crime; to make justice more healing, and, ideally transformative; and to reduce the likelihood of future offences."[23]

Victim-Offender Mediation

In the practice of *victim-offender mediation,* the key participants are the victim, the offender and at least one, if not two, skilled mediators. Susan Sharpe states, "The recognition that victims and offenders must face one another in order for justice to emerge between them is undoubtedly as old as human civilization, but it was lost from official judicial proceedings over the past 200 years."[24] Resurrecting this practice fosters healing, connection, and often empowerment for both victim and offender. Victim-offender mediation rests on the premise that *a person* has been harmed rather than the state. It helps restore and repair the loss experienced by the victim, and the offender is held accountable in specific ways that speak to the damage he or she has inflicted.

---

22. Magnani and Wray, *Beyond Prisons*, 164.
23. Sharpe, *Restorative Justice*, 20.
24. Ibid., 24.

In this practice of restorative justice, trained mediators facilitate the face-to-face meeting between victim and offender. In this way feelings can be expressed and decisions reached as to the best means, agreeable to all, to repair the harm that has been done. The initial focus is, of course, on the victim, who has the opportunity to directly address the offender in regard to the effects of the crime, whether those effects are physical, emotional, or economic. As it is generally understood that the tendency of any victim is to blame oneself, such a direct face-to-face dialogue provides the victim with the opportunity to ask the offender questions as to motivations for the crime and in this way helps the victim to heal from the trauma of the violation.

As for the offender, such face-to-face confrontation allows for an explanation of what may have precipitated the offense, expression of this individual's feelings in regard to his or her actions and the resulting harm. In *Changing Lenses*, Howard Zehr, speaking of his own work in victim-offender mediation affirms, "by being encouraged to take responsibility for making things right—they are held directly accountable for what they have done. Because they are real participants rather than bystanders, they too can experience empowerment."[25]

In this particular restorative justice practice, members of the community are not usually involved. While it is possible for the victim or offender to invite a family member or friend to attend, that person does not take part in the dialogue but rather serves as a supportive presence. What often proves most powerful is the dialogue for "the small number of participants can deepen the emotional intensity of the topic, making it easier for each party to speak from the heart. As this happens, much of what is restored is each party's humanity in the other's eyes."[26]

Victim-offender mediation has most often been used for what would be termed minor crimes. It has also, however, with the assistance of specially trained mediators, been used in more serious and violent crimes. Sometimes it is the community police who initiate the referral for such mediation and at other times it is initiated within the courts. It has also been utilized within the prison setting itself to facilitate healing of severe offenses. In whatever the setting, the opportunity for healing and making things right is of primary importance. In this way it reflects the biblical vision of shalom. Noting that the church played a key role

25. Zehr, *Changing Lenses*, 162.

26. Sharpe, *Restorative Justice*, 26.

in the growth of victim-offender mediation, Howard Zehr states, "the church's role is critical" and if such a practice "is to survive as a catalyst for change, the church must remain involved."[27]

Community Conferencing

The restorative justice practice of *community conferencing* also has its roots in centuries-old ways of solving human conflict and wrongdoing. While it is rather new to restorative justice practices in North America, it is steadily gaining ground. In its more recent resurrection as a restorative justice practice, it was known as family group conferencing and took hold among indigenous populations first in New Zealand and later in Australia as a response to the growing numbers of juvenile offenders. Growing out of the New Zealand Maori tradition of family involvement with a youthful offender and seeking accountability for the offence, family and government joined together to work for a more positive resolution to youth crime. "In 1989, the New Zealand Parliament passed legislation that made family group conferences the standard way of responding to young people's criminal behavior. Youth court became the exception, not the rule."[28]

The term *family group conferencing* was the term initially used to describe this practice because indeed it did involve the offender's family in assisting to repair the harm inflicted. However, as the practice evolved to include adult offenders, *community conferencing* is now the term most often used for such practices, as those involved in the process may not necessarily be the offender's family but rather individuals who are supportive of the offender and seek to help the offender make things right. Regardless of the terminology, the underlying values are nevertheless the same: healing from and repairing the harm inflicted.

Similar to victim-offender mediation, the role of dialogue is of crucial importance. The opportunity to express feelings, ask questions, seek understanding, and formulate a resolution for repairing the harm—all facilitate the process of healing and shalom. All those present—the offender, the victim and those who are there to offer support—are invited to participate. In this way, community conferencing differs in one important way from victim-offender mediation. The presence of family,

27. Zehr, *Changing Lenses,* 173–74.
28. Sharpe, *Restorative Justice,* 30.

friends, or members of the community provide for what Braithwaite refers to as reintegrative shaming. Here, the clear acknowledgement of wrongdoing not only to the victim, but also to individuals who share an emotional connection to the offender, and perhaps a biological one as well, helps to build a more healthy conscience within the offender. Those individuals who have come to support the offender, while clearly and emphatically disapproving of the criminal behavior, simultaneously make a clear distinction between their disapproval of the offending action and the offender as an individual person. Their supportive presence, their expressed belief in the basic human goodness of the offender and his or her potential to make things right and to continue to live in right relationship with self and others, allows the offender to gain a clearer understanding of the effects of the harm inflicted, to reestablish healthy connections to the community, and to remain connected to the community in a positive way. While the broader participation that is part of this type of restorative justice practice also carries with it the challenge of greater time and energy required for careful listening to all participants, if undertaken with care and wisdom, it too provides an opportunity for much healing and restoration.

Community Peacemaking Circles

The third restorative justice practice, *community peacemaking circles*, is rooted in ancient wisdom practices of aboriginal peoples in Canada and the American Indians in the United States. In 1991 it was revived by a few judges in Canada who were particularly concerned with juvenile offenders, and in 1996 it spread to the United States where a pilot project was initiated in Minnesota.[29] While there are a few variations of the peacemaking circle such as the healing circle, which brings people together with the hope of resolving conflict before it evolves into criminal actions, and the sentencing circle, which determines, by means of consensus involving all participants, a court sentence that will be implemented, the community peacemaking circle differs from victim-offender mediation and community conferencing in a few important ways. With regard to community peacemaking circles, Susan Sharpe states, "Circles take the perspective that criminal behavior is a symptom of a deeper problem. What must be solved is the underlying problem, not just the

---

29. Bazemore and Umbreit, "Four Restorative Conferencing Models," 233.

behavior. The symptom indicates an imbalance somewhere within. If the symptom is treated but the imbalance is not corrected, disease is likely to develop and may cause permanent damage."[30] In this practice, not only is the offender held accountable and required to repair the harm inflicted, but there is strong emphasis on helping the offender stay on a straight path, with the family and community taking clear responsibility towards righting the wrongs that have contributed to the offence. "From this perspective, justice is stable and workable only when victim, offender, family, and community are in proper relation to each other."[31]

In all three of these practices, the victim is involved and is given a voice as well as influence in the outcome. The offender is able to understand, in a direct and meaningful way, the impact of his or her offence and to take direct and active responsibility toward repairing the harm. The very practice itself helps to heal the harm, fosters understanding among all participants, and deepens the awareness of our shared humanity. The victim is not relegated to the sidelines nor is the offender simply banished to prison. Both are reintegrated back into the community, and the community, rather than being left with a weakened sense of autonomy, is actually strengthened. As Sharpe affirms, "Victim-offender mediation, community conferencing, and community peacemaking circles all challenge the notion that the state is better equipped to deal with crime than community members are."[32]

A CHANGE OF PHILOSOPHY AND PRACTICE

Restorative justice provides a vastly different perspective on criminal behavior; it requires that we revamp and revolutionize our attitudes toward crime, redefining both our understanding and practices of justice. "Restorative justice challenges the fundamental philosophy of the current justice system, and asks community members to do something quite different from what happens in the courts."[33] In doing so, it empowers victims by giving them a voice to express their pain, their anguish, their needs; it empowers offenders by holding them accountable, *not* to the state, but rather to the victim, allowing them to take direct responsibility

30. Sharpe, *Restorative Justice*, 39.

31. Ibid., 39.

32. Ibid., 37.

33. Ibid., i.

in repairing the harm they have caused; and thereby, it empowers communities to re-create the healing and harmony necessary for restoring right relationship.

Healing and harmony, shalom, making things right, must necessarily be a primary value, if not *the* underlying foundation of human living. While disharmony and disconnection are a condition of our humanity, restoring right relationship must necessarily be the underlying motivation of human living. Somewhere, in the deepest recesses of every human heart is the yearning for healing and harmony, for mercy and forgiveness, for communion and reunion, for reconciliation and wholeness. In the Judeo-Christian tradition, God speaks to our yearning and invites us into right relationship; God invites us into shalom.

QUESTIONS FOR REFLECTION AND DISCUSSION

1. How does restorative justice challenge you? What is at stake when we embrace restorative versus retributive justice? How would such movement impact your community?

2. What have your experiences been with the prison system? How have you been personally impacted by crime and the criminal justice system? How has your church community been impacted?

3. How do we want those individuals who have experienced imprisonment to be when they return to us? Take a few moments to compare the effects of retributive versus restorative justice on the perpetrator, the victim, and the community.

4. Out of your own experience, can you speak to the effects of disintegrative shaming as contrasted with reintegrative shaming? In what ways are you in need of healing and restoration? Take a moment and imagine what healing would feel and look like. What would be necessary to foster this kind of healing in your life? How would the Biblical concept of shalom assist in such healing?

5. Consider the attitudes and values of retributive punishment compared with those of restorative justice as practiced by Jesus of Nazareth. Read John 8:3–11 and Luke 19:1–10. What steps might we take to educate our own faith community as well as our larger community in the practices of restorative justice?

3

A Theology of Mutual Relation: A Vision for Healing

*Only love—the embodied commitment to struggle together for right,
mutual relation—can work the miracles required to create justice in the
midst of exploitation and peace in the midst of violence.*

—CARTER HEYWARD, *SAVING JESUS FROM THOSE WHO ARE RIGHT*

IF INDEED, GOD IS always calling us home, always calling us into right
relationship with self, with others, with Godself, it would seem that
the Divine Source of our being, the Divine Source of our universe, is
calling us into a shared relationship, a mutual relationship, a human-di-
vine relationship of care, concern, and compassion for our life together
here on this earth. This chapter will consider a relational theology in the
context of both retributive justice and restorative justice.

DISCONNECTION FOSTERED
BY A RETRIBUTIVE JUSTICE SYSTEM

The prison system as it currently exists serves to isolate and alienate individuals. While it does so in the name of justice and the purported need
for protection of society, the result is a disconnection of persons, not only
from the larger human community, but because of the need to wall off the
pain and shame of such alienating punishment, there is also a disconnection from one's self within one's deep core of being. When an individual is
disconnected from self and others, to a large degree, that individual is also
disconnected from Godself. Retributive punishment reflects authoritarian
power relations that only deepen disconnection, and as theologian Carter

Heyward observes, "Evil is rooted in non-mutual authoritarian relational dynamics, that, in the real world, are usually patriarchal."[1]

CONNECTION FOSTERED
BY A RESTORATIVE JUSTICE SYSTEM

In contrast, restorative justice with its foundational principles of righting the wrongs between human persons and the human community provides for connection rather than disconnection, for healing rather than harming, for allowing for the possibility of good to flourish rather than further destruction and evil stemming from deepening disconnection. The roots in Scripture for such a practice of justice are not only to be found in the Old Testament concept of shalom but also as noted by Howard Zehr, "Jesus continues and expands this theme of covenant justice. He focuses on the recovery of wholeness in community with one another and with God. In the New Testament as in the Old, justice has a relational focus."[2]

DISCONNECTION AND CONNECTION WITHIN
A THEOLOGY OF MUTUAL RELATION

Our essence as human beings is relational. Our birth into life on this earth is grounded in relation, grounded first in God out of the divine mystery of our creation, and then immediately grounded in connection with other human beings. In his book, *Reconciliation: The Ubuntu Theology of Desmond Tutu*, author Michael Battle states, "Indeed, such human interdependence is built into our very creation by our being created in God's image, our common *imago Dei*."[3] Whenever this connection is disrupted or distorted, our sense of self and worth is threatened. Such threat may be momentary and minor or it may be enduring and exacting. According to psychologists Jean Baker Miller and Irene Pierce Stiver, "disconnections are what we experience when we feel cut off from those with whom we share a relationship."[4] Severe disconnection results in a sense of isolation, shame, and a diminished sense of self-worth. Indeed, Miller and Stiver "believe that the most terrifying and destruc-

1. Heyward, *Saving Jesus*, 77.

2. Zehr, "Retributive Justice, Restorative Justice," 78.

3. Battle, *Reconciliation*, 40.

4. Miller and Stiver, *Healing Connection*, 11.

tive feeling that a person can experience is psychological isolation—the feeling that one is locked out of the possibility of human connection and of being powerless to change the situation."[5]

Connection, on the other hand, energizes and empowers; it fosters growth in self-awareness, deepens mutual regard between self and others, and enhances self-worth. Connection speaks of reciprocity, mutuality, and interdependence. Truly, the epitome of connection may best be understood in the African concept of *ubuntu*, which understands that "individuals have no existence apart from their relations with other persons."[6] It is here then, in such connection and community with one another and with God, that healing and wholeness may be found in the midst of our human failings and transgressions.

GOD REMAINS RELATIONAL IN THE MIDST OF HUMAN WRONGDOING

Human mistakes, human sin, human wrongdoing are an inevitable part of the human condition; it comes with the territory, and in the Judeo-Christian tradition, the story of Adam and Eve and their disobedience forms the framework for the tales of the human journey with God. In the earliest chapters of Genesis, humankind is confronted with punishment. The source of Adam and Eve's "sin" and their vulnerability and accountability have been subjects of theological discussion for centuries. The consequence of punishment by God, however, is generally considered a natural outcome for these two children in paradise and their refusal to listen to their all-knowing, all-powerful parent. While it might seem that their banishment by God from the Garden of Eden is a rather severe punishment, it is important to remember that even as God inflicts punishment, God does not alienate them, abuse them, or abandon them. Indeed, God continues to journey with them and even bless them as Eve testifies with the birth of her first son, Cain, declaring, "I have produced a man with the help of the Lord" (Gen 4:1).

Here again, it is in the life of Cain where God's punishment will be inflicted once more. Here too, the source of Cain's "sin" has been the subject of theological discussion. Surely in this instance, with Cain's murder of his brother Abel, God has an indisputable right to punish. Even Cain

5. Ibid., 72.

6. Battle, *Reconciliation*, 50.

himself expects to be killed in retaliation for his act saying, "I shall be a fugitive and a wanderer on the earth, and anyone who meets me may kill me" (Gen 4:14). God, however, does not seek retaliation in punishment but instead marks Cain so that *no one* shall kill him. Moreover, God asserts "whoever kills Cain will suffer a sevenfold vengeance" (Gen 4:15). While God's anger with the "sins" of human creatures is visible and palpable, God's punishments allow for human lives to go forward with their experience of their separation from God being the definitive burden of their punishment.

For even in God's heartache and disappointment with the wicked and evil ways of human beings and God's decision to blot out *all* that Godself has created, there is still hope for redemption in the person of Noah who finds favor with God, and so God relents and reconsiders the decision to destroy all life. It seems that in the midst of punishment, God will ultimately be rational, reasonable, and restorative. God remains connected to us; God continues to hold us in relationship. Scholar Eugene Peterson in his book *The Message*, a version of the Bible in contemporary language, confirms this in his introduction to the Book of Genesis when he states, "No matter what we do, whether good or bad, we continue to be part of everything that God is doing."[7] From the very beginning then, God is relational, and the divine-human relation is established as the foundation of human life on earth.

NONMUTUAL RELATIONS AS SOURCE OF EVIL

How then has this foundational divine-human relationship of mutuality and connection, of healing and restoration been lost? How has it been marginalized? Just as it is helpful and necessary to consider the history of punishment as a means of understanding how we have arrived at our present system of retributive punishment, so too, it is helpful and necessary to consider certain aspects in the history of our Judeo-Christian heritage that foster and breed disconnection, serving to spawn more harm and evil within the human community.

As noted previously by Carter Heyward, evil is rooted in nonmutual, authoritarian relations, usually patriarchal, and herein may lie those aspects of our spiritual heritage that have dislodged us from our true, essential, mutual relationship with God, self, and other. Behind the screen

---

7. Peterson, *Message*, 19.

of patriarchy, the forces of redemptive violence, domination, controlling power, and the God-images contained within such forces, wield a powerful influence on our capacity to live in right relationship to self and to other, as well as on our capacity to create that beloved community, the kingdom of God here on earth. These forces greatly influence our perceptions of punishment, of what constitutes justice, and whether our practices of justice will be retributive or restorative.

A retributive justice system utilizes authoritarian, controlling, dominating, power-over relations rather than shared, respectful, mutual, power-with relations as practiced in restorative justice. Here, it may be helpful to consider the roots of power as domination. In his book, *Engaging the Powers*, theologian Walter Wink provides an in-depth understanding of the domination system and the violence such a system breeds.

In the early civilization of the Babylonian city-states, constant warfare and chaos were a continual threat to human civilization. The myth that grounded this culture, dating back to 1250 BCE, is the mythology of the Enuma Elish. In this myth, the younger gods plot to kill the elder gods. When the god Apsu is murdered, his wife Tiamat seeks revenge. The younger gods look to their youngest, Marduk to save them. While Marduk agrees, his price for success is high, i.e. he will be given the place of eminent power among the gods. Indeed, "he catches Tiamat in a net, drives an evil wind down her throat, shoots an arrow that bursts her distended belly, and pierces her heart; he then splits her skull with a club and scatters her blood in out-of-the-way places. He stretches out her corpse full length, and from it creates the cosmos."[8] In this Babylonian myth, the act of creation is embedded in violence. It is through violence and domination that life is redeemed. Evil originates before the creation of the material world.

The biblical myth is in opposition to this violent myth, for creation is inherently good created by a good God. Good precedes evil; there is no violence. Indeed, neither are part of the original creation of the cosmos. Rather, sin or evil results out of free decisions by creatures. Sin or evil is now a problem requiring a solution.[9] While there are key differences between these mythologies of creation, nevertheless the Babylonian myth of redemptive violence permeates both the history of Judaism and Christianity. According to Wink, the real religion of America is

8. Wink, *Engaging the Powers*, 13.
9. Ibid., 14.

not Christianity, but rather, it is the religion of Babylon with its myth of redemptive violence. States Wink, "Violence was for the religion of ancient Mesopotamia what love was for Jesus: the central dynamic of existence."[10]

The myth of redemptive violence has as its underlying foundation revenge, power as domination, and the reigning motif of violence. So too, the present retributive justice system has as its underlying foundation revenge, power as domination, and the reigning motif of violence. It is destructive because "the distinctive feature of the myth is the victory of order over chaos by means of violence."[11] Confronting this myth embedded in the retributive justice system is essential in the movement towards restorative justice. For as Wink states, "Jesus taught the love of enemies but Babylonian religion taught their extermination,"[12] and if we are to transform our practices of justice, it is necessary to understand the roots of our attitudes and behaviors.

While it was Jesus who embodied God's domination-free order and seemed for a time to offer an alternative way of nonviolent love, eventually the "Domination System"[13] proved too powerful. The Christian Church moved to the very hierarchy and violence Jesus had rejected. The Christian Church under the aegis of the Domination System has been but one of its many structures and institutions and the prison organization is yet another. According to Wink, the metaphor for the myth of redemptive violence is "a fortress. Its symbol is not the cross but a rod of iron. Its offer is not forgiveness but victory. Its good news is not the unconditional love of enemies but their final liquidation."[14] The present prison system in its mode of retributive justice, for the most part, only serves to perpetuate more violence, even as it claims to be redemptive in administering justice. Psychiatrist James Gilligan, out of his direct work within prisons states, "The very conditions that occur regularly in most prisons may force prisoners to engage in acts of serious violence in order to avoid being mutilated, raped, or murdered themselves."[15] The myth of redemptive violence continues to flourish amidst the spirit of retributive punishment.

10. Ibid., 13.
11. Ibid., 16.
12. Ibid., 13.
13. Ibid., 9.
14. Ibid., 30.
15. Gilligan, *Violence*, 163.

THE ROOTS OF POWER RELATIONS

Underlying this myth are the motivating forces of dominating power and control. These forces also have historical roots whereby a domination system of social and economic organization reigns supreme. If we are to understand the roots of power relations of dominance and control it is necessary to trace our steps back to the civilizations of Mesopotamia. Previous to this time in history, human relationships were oriented toward mutuality, reciprocity, and interdependence. People lived in small enclaves or villages and together hunted and gathered food; relationships were essentially egalitarian. Within a clan or village, decisions were made in a spirit of democracy; there was a spirit of genuine interdependence and mutual relationship. With the domestication of animals and the development of agriculture, however, there was a major shift in human relationships. Theologian and social psychologist Diarmuid O'Murchu states, "It was the agricultural revolution in the tenth-century BC that undermined an otherwise wholistic vision, creating the competitive and exploitative differentiation that has bedeviled civilization ever since."[16] With the rise of city states around the years 6000 to 5000 BC villages grew into small cities, and land, rather than being shared, became a commodity. Of key importance at this time was the introduction of land irrigation systems and as Starhawk, in her book, *Truth or Dare*, states, "irrigation made some land enormously more productive, and therefore more valuable than other land. Some groups and individuals became rich; others were gradually made poor."[17] The unequal status of the land resulted in unequal status among the people, providing some with more wealth and consequently more power.

THE DOMINATION SYSTEM AND THE POWERS AS EMBODIED IN THE PRISON INSTITUTION

Indeed, as Walter Wink notes in his book, *The Powers That Be*, "social systems became rigidly hierarchal, authoritarian, and patriarchal."[18] The Domination System became entrenched, characterized by "unjust economic relations, oppressive political relations, biased race relations,

16. O'Murchu, *Our World in Transition*, 66.

17. Starhawk, *Truth or Dare*, 38.

18. Wink, *Powers That Be*, 40.

patriarchal gender relations, hierarchal power relations, and the use of violence to maintain them all."[19]

Truly, the present prison institution embodies all of these, utilizing cheap and free prison labor, for, "not only are the jobs of U.S. workers being moved by corporations to lower costing labor in Third World countries, but increasingly they are being moved into U.S. prisons."[20] Furthermore, impoverished minorities are being imprisoned in greater and greater numbers, with the fastest growing group of the prison population being women, whose numbers inside prison walls have doubled in the past twenty years.[21] The Domination System, with its use of abusive, authoritarian power relations, is evil incarnate, for it generates and perpetuates humans who are disordered and disconnected from their own humanity, their fellow humans, and the world.

Contained within the structures and institutions of the Domination System are the Powers. The structures and institutions are the Powers, reflecting the visible, outer manifestation of an inner spiritual reality. As Walter Wink describes them, "the Powers are simultaneously the outer and inner aspects of one and the same indivisible concretion of power."[22] Indeed, the ancient worldview of the "Principalities and Powers" held an essential truth, which was that political, economic, and cultural institutions embody an actual spiritual nature.[23] Just as an individual person is both the outer manifestation of his or her physical body *and* the inner reality of mind, heart, and spirit, so also there is both the inner and outer manifestations of our structures and institutions whether they be nations, governments, or in the context of the subject matter at hand, the institution of the prison.

Wink is careful to emphasize that to see the Powers as only evil is one-sided and holds its own dangers. Just as human beings are good, just as human beings are fallen, just as human beings must be redeemed, the Powers are also good, the Powers have also fallen, and the Powers must also be redeemed.[24] Human beings are rooted in God's good creation and so too are human structures and institutions. Human structures and

---

19. Ibid., 39.
20. Burton-Rose, *Celling of America*, 101.
21. Reiman, *Rich Get Rich*, xi.
22. Wink, *Naming the Powers*, 107.
23. Wink, *Engaging the Powers*, 6.
24. Ibid., 10.

institutions are necessary and useful for human living, preventing both chaos and anarchy. Their inner aspect, their spirituality if you will, is good to the extent it serves the well-being and flourishing of human growth and actualization; it is evil to the extent it fosters disarray, disconnection, and disrespect for the creation of God's beloved community here on earth.

What is imperative is to discern whether the inner spirituality of any outward manifestation of reality, be it person, place, or thing, is healthy and whole, reflecting the goodness of created order, or broken and diseased, reflecting the malevolence of created order. If God's created order is inherently good, then we human beings as part of that created order are inherently good, and the institutions we have created are inherently good to the extent that all serve the divine purpose of creating community, love, and justice on this earth.

In discerning the inner spirituality of the prison institution as it presently exists, it is unequivocally clear that it is diseased, for it breeds disconnection, generates rage and hatred, and fuels oppression. How can such a system be anything less than diseased when it fosters further racial and gender discrimination; ignores physical, emotional, and spiritual needs; inflicts maltreatment and isolation of individuals, causing additional alienation with severe psychological trauma; and treats not only the prisoners but their families in humiliating and degrading ways, relating to both from an abusive authoritarian stance. If one is awake, alert, and attentive, one can sense and feel the diseased spirituality of the prison institution through the simple action of walking through those prison doors. The words of Carter Heyward ring true: "Injustice, or oppression, is both source and consequence of evil—non-mutual power relations of domination and control."[25] In contrast to the diseased spirituality of retributive justice, restorative justice in its effort to promote healing, reconnection, and restoration among individuals and the human community may well provide a prelude towards the transformation of the present retributive justice system.

Yet Wink is very clear when he affirms, "any attempt to transform a social system without addressing both its spirituality and its outer forms is doomed to failure."[26] He provides an excellent example of this when he describes the United States civil rights movement of the sixties and

25. Heyward, *Saving Jesus*, 55.
26. Wink, *Engaging the Powers*, 10.

Martin Luther King Jr.'s ability to speak to the issue of racism, both its outer structure and its inner spirit as it lived within the nation itself. Wink states,

> He resolutely refused to treat racism as a political issue only; he insisted that it be seen also as a moral and spiritual sickness. He did not attack the soul of America, but appealed to its most profound depths. His confrontational tactics were attempts to address that soul. He called a nation to repent, and significant numbers did. In the process, the spirit of the nation itself began to change.[27]

CONFRONTING THE SPIRITUALITY OF THE PRISON INSTITUTION

Wink emphasizes clearly that, "only by confronting the spirituality of an institution and its concretions can the total entity be transformed, and that requires a kind of spiritual discernment and praxis that the materialistic ethos in which we live knows nothing about."[28] Spiritual discernment and praxis, however, speak of living in the awareness of the Spirit that lives and moves within and among us. Such awareness is not readily acknowledged in the postmodern milieu in which we in the Western world live, which places such great value on that which can be quantified, objectified, visualized, contained, and possessed. The machine imagery of Sir Isaac Newton—which helped to explain how the world worked in the seventeenth century and in turn led to the metaphor of the world as a giant clock and God as the great clockmaker who set the world in motion—continues to wield enormous influence in our thinking and behavior over three hundred years later, despite how enlightened we like to believe we are. In her book, *Leadership and the New Science*, author Margaret Wheatley notes how materialistic Newtonian science is for, "it seeks to comprehend the world by focusing on what can be known through our physical senses. Anything *real* has visible and tangible physical form."[29] The new science, however, as discovered in the arena of quantum physics, rather than seeing the world as a clock/machine with its various parts, sees the world as a whole system and "attention is given to relationships within

---

27. Wink, *Naming the Powers*, 129.
28. Wink, *Engaging the Powers*, 10.
29. Wheatley, *Leadership and the New Science*, 10.

those networks."[30] The unseen, mysterious connections between all entities within the created order of life on earth, from our visible and tangible human bodies to the invisible and intangible atoms and molecules that comprise those bodies provide evidence for the complex interrelatedness of all of life. States Wheatley, "These unseen *connections* between what were previously thought to be separate entities are the fundamental ingredient of all creation. In the quantum world, *relationship* is the key determiner of everything."[31] The new science then, may in time, set in motion a movement toward a new theology, toward new metaphors of God in relation with all of creation, rather than God over and above creation. Indeed, as theologian Walter Wink emphasizes, "What is at stake is a veritable revolution in our God-images. Nothing could be more crucial, because *our images of God create us.*"[32]

IMAGES OF GOD AND THE PRISON INSTITUTION

Certainly, our images of God are readily reflected in the ordinary and frequent language we use in speaking and singing about God, such as God the Father, God as Lord, God as King, Heavenly Father, Lord of Lords, King of Kings, Almighty and All-Powerful God. Theologian Sallie McFague in her book, *Models of God*, asserts, "the metaphors of God as king, ruler, lord, master, and governor, and the concepts that accompany them of God as absolute, complete, transcendent, and omnipotent permit no sense of mutuality, shared responsibility, reciprocity, and love (except in the sense of gratitude)."[33] The almighty father as ruler, king, and master expects strict obedience to his authority and exacts severe punishment with the infraction of his rules and laws. From a theological perspective, it is possible that our images of God may well influence our thinking and behavior with regard to wrongdoing and punishment. In his own work within the prisons, Gilligan has observed that criminal trials are representative of the Last Judgment, prisons are modeled after hell, the judges after God, and the correctional officers after the devil.[34] Indeed, he acknowledges that this is clearly reflected in

30. Ibid., 10.
31. Ibid., 11.
32. Wink, *Engaging the Powers*, 48.
33. McFague, *Models of God*, 19.
34. Gilligan, *Violence*, 159.

paintings of the Italian Renaissance.[35] While this may prove unsettling and discomforting to many in our postmodern world, it is confirmed by others. In her treatise, *Punishment in the Scripture and Tradition of Judaism, Christianity, and Islam*, the Reverend Virginia Mackey states, "The theology of a people invariably influences the structures which emerge to cope with situations of conflict. If we are unaware of such influence then the current structures and practices of punishment remain fixed, unquestioned and unchallenged."[36]

While a new theology and new metaphors of God arising from the new science may appear heretical, it is essential to remember that, so too, at one time the scientific concepts of Galileo were considered both revolutionary and heretical, yet they forever changed humankind's view of both God and the world. Indeed, there is a new worldview emerging, one which incorporates the understandings of the new science in combination with philosophy, psychology, and theology. Walter Wink refers to this new worldview as an integral worldview and asserts that all of reality has an outer and inner aspect, an outward physical manifestation that we see and an inner spirituality that we sense.[37] It is essential that we hold both together simultaneously; it is essential that we remember the relationship of both. For in all of the created order, in the very universe itself, in both the divine created order and the human created order, there is a connection, a relationship, an inherent mutuality. God and heaven are not *up there* while human creatures and earth are *down here*; spirit and matter coexist concurrently as surely in human creatures as in human institutions.

CREATING RELATIONAL IMAGES OF GOD

While aspects of awe and reverence to a Source and Power above and beyond ourselves as human creatures are essential attitudes in our ability to live with care and compassion for all of creation, aspects of fear and domination implicit in such images all too often restrict our movement toward deeper and more encompassing images *of* God, thus restricting our movement toward a deeper and more encompassing relationship *with* God. For just as God is active in all of creation, it necessarily follows

35. Ibid., 158.
36. Mackey, *Punishment in the Scripture*, 48.
37. Wink, *Engaging the Powers*, 6.

that God is active within each of us, for each one of us is part of that creation. Other images of God that could assist us in moving beyond the solely patriarchal, monarchal, images of God as father, ruler, and judge might be of God as mother, companion, healer, friend, and sustainer. These images hold different understandings of God that might enable us to relate to God, to self, to others, in a spirit of love and understanding, in a spirit of care and compassion, in a spirit of genuine mutual relation. Such images could help us move from a retributive position of justice as vengeance to a restorative posture of justice as shalom.

We are born in relation, human being to human being. Just as God's creational power is in mutual relation, with the Spirit of God's power being birthed through us, so too, our creational power is in our mutual relation with self, with other, with God, and with our world. Affirming this awareness allows for understandings of God in mutual relationship with us as human beings and with all of the created order. It would seem then that our failure to grow in our God-images prevents us from living in right relationship with self, other, and God. For as Carter Heyward notes, a model of "God over humanity, humanity under God, forces locked in opposition—distorts the integrity of creation and tears at the relational fabric of our lives."[38]

Such a model represents power-over rather than power-with. Such power comes from above. Such power is not shared. With regard to punishment and imprisonment, the state holds power over the individual and the community by means of the prison institution. In the face of the institution, the prisoners are powerless, the families and friends of the prisoners are powerless, and the community is powerless. So too with God—we all too often believe we are powerless because our image is of God over us rather than God with us. Both reflect relationships of domination, and McFague is quick to remind us that "power as domination has been and still is a central feature of the Western view of God."[39] It may well be that transformation from a retributive system of justice to a restorative system of justice will require an awareness of how our images of God are indeed harnessed to our attitudes and practices of punishment. With such awareness comes the acknowledgement of the need to work with God images in order to nurture mutual relationships of care and compassion, of justice and mercy, of understanding and for-

38. Heyward, *Saving Jesus*, 100.
39. McFague, *Models of God*, 16.

giveness with self, with others, with God and our world. In her book, *Models of God*, McFague considers images of God as mother, lover, and friend, and suggests that all "are united in that each points to a desire for union; each, in a different way, draws attention to the interrelatedness and interdependence of all life."[40] Recognizing our interrelatedness and interdependence with God, with all others, and with life, and working together to conceive and create images of God that foster more mutual relation helps to insure against a punitive, vengeful reaction to crime, and helps instead to promote a more compassionate, restorative response to criminal behavior.

SOCIAL POWER IN THE CONTEXT OF A RELATIONAL THEOLOGY

Presently, however, the power of the state and the prison institution is the power of domination, and the power of domination precludes mutuality, promoting instead, discord and disconnection. What is essential is to understand that power relations of domination and control are not limited to the prison institution. The root of such relations are situated in the very fabric of society and such relations permeate the very existence of our day-to-day living. Indeed, they are so deeply embedded that all too often they go unnoticed and remain all too often unchallenged. In his book, *Engaging the Powers*, Walter Wink repeatedly refers to such power relations of domination and control as the Domination System.[41] Indeed, the Babylonian myth of creation, with its ethos of redemptive violence, the Powers, and the Domination System are all interrelated, and if we are to create a new theology, a theology of mutual relation, it is imperative that we understand the roots of the forces that impact our human relationships and institutions, including the institution of the prison. It is essential to recognize that a theology of mutual relation is not just about our relationships personally, one on one, one to another. Rather, it is both interpersonal—social *and* political. For as Carter Heyward states, "a relational theology puts a study, or analysis, of social power at the center of theological reflection."[42]

40. Ibid., 92.
41. Wink, *Engaging the Powers*, 46.
42. Heyward, *Saving Jesus*, 63.

A theology of mutual relation in the context of the prison institution needs to take into account issues of class, race, and gender. To attempt to practice prison ministry without any understanding of the underlying social, political, and economic factors bound up in that sphere is to render such ministry minimally effective if not totally ineffective. As Reverend Virginia Mackey notes, "Most Americans do not have a strong sense of consequence. They do not view the problem of crime in its social context, nor do they examine the socio-economic genesis of most so-called criminal activity."[43] Yet, given the dramatic and profound changes that have taken place in imprisonment in the United States in the last twenty years, the sociopolitical and economic factors inherent in the system are clearly evident and impossible to ignore.

The multitude of individuals now imprisoned represents the lowest economic class in United States society. In other words, the majority of prisoners are poor, and there is a direct correlation between the laws established by those in positions of power and privilege and those whose lives are impoverished and consequently impacted by such laws. One needs only pause momentarily to consider that the politicians who create criminal laws, the lawyers who prosecute individuals who break the laws, and the judges who sentence such individuals, are all representative of upper-class, privileged society. Such a nonmutual relationship serves to maintain the vested interests of the status quo. In his book, *The Rich Get Richer and the Poor Get Prison*, author Jeffrey Reiman states, "Between crimes that are characteristically committed by poor people (street crimes) and those characteristically committed by the well-off (white collar and corporate crimes), the system treats the former much more harshly than the latter, even when the crimes of the well off take more money from the public or cause more death and injury than the crimes of the poor."[44]

Additionally, the issue of class is inextricably yoked to the issue of race. Just as black Americans are disproportionately poor, so too are they disproportionately represented in the prison system. Given the burgeoning numbers of prisoners convicted for nonviolent, usually drug-related offenses, "arrests of blacks for illicit drug possession or dealing have skyrocketed in recent years, rising way out of proportion to drug arrests for whites—though research shows no greater drug use among blacks than among whites."[45] The correlation here, as noted by Reiman,

43. Mackey, *Punishment in the Scripture*, 51.

44. Reiman, *Rich Get Richer*, 145.

45. Ibid., 112.

is that drug arrests are more easily made in inner-city ghettos where there is less likelihood of concealment around such activity, and poverty is clearly a mark of inner-city neighborhoods.[46]

Also critical is that, amidst the burgeoning numbers of those imprisoned for nonviolent, drug-related offenses, women comprise the fastest growing population, and here too, class and race are readily apparent. Tragically, most of these women have children who become innocent victims of the prison system's nonmutual relations of dominance and control, and they are often separated from their mothers at great distances and for extended periods of time. Related to the issue of gender, it is a fact that most of these women have histories of sexual, physical, and emotional abuse.[47] Their lives are a glaring reflection of lack of opportunity, lack of education; a glaring reflection of the inequities encased within the Domination System.

Then there are the economics of the prison institution, which are clearly part of the Domination System. With the "tough on crime" legislative policies enacted during the decade of the nineties, the "three strikes and you're out" strategies adopted in many states, and the new drug enforcement laws, the prison population soared to unprecedented numbers. State budgets, to say nothing of the prison facilities themselves, were stretched to capacity. The ensuing result was that the privatization of prisons became the most practical, prudent, and pragmatic course of action. What transpired throughout the following months and years was the growth of what is now termed the *prison-industrial complex*. Prisons have become big business, with big name financiers such as Smith Barney and Merrill Lynch investing in the building of prisons.[48] In his article, "Campus Activism Defeats Multinational's Prison Profiteering," grassroots campaign organizer Kevin Pranis states, "Recognizing an opportunity to make fortunes off the backs of prisoners and their families, Corporate America—including architects, bankers, building contractors, and telephone companies—lined up at the prison trough."[49] It becomes obvious then that "Corporate America" has a stake in crime and punishment, for crime and punishment hold the promise of clear and considerable profit.

46. Ibid., 113.
47. Herivel, "Wreaking Medical Mayhem," 176.
48. Reiman, *Rich Get Richer*, 162.
49. Pranis, "Campus Activism," 156.

JESUS AS MODEL OF MUTUAL RELATION

As discussed here, exploitation, domination, power, and control are all marks of the prison institution as well as of the many other systems and institutions in which we work and live. The Domination System is alive and well, thriving as well now as it did centuries ago, and it is this system of domination that Jesus of Nazareth challenged in word and deed, for in no sense whatsoever was Jesus exploitative, domineering, or controlling. In no sense whatsoever was Jesus triumphal, monarchial, or patriarchal. On the contrary, in every sense, Jesus was relational. Indeed, he modeled a theology of mutual relation in every possible way, par excellence!

With God, with his Abba, Jesus lived in mutuality, in intimacy and immediacy, where the Spirit of God was as close to Jesus as his own breath. And it was the shared power of the Spirit offered as invitation to *all* to live in right relation to self, other, and God that was foundational to the ministry of Jesus. As Delores Williams affirms in her book, *Sisters in the Wilderness,* "it can be claimed that these right relationships he advocated challenged the injustice characterized by oppressed-oppressor relations. Jesus' ministerial (or pastoral) vision brought justice and care to relationships."[50] In his teachings, his healings, his parables, Jesus lived his vision of right relationship as he witnessed to the power of the Spirit moving within him through his compassion, healing, mercy, and love for the oppressed, the wounded, and the tortured.

However, not only did Jesus witness to mutual and right relationship with God, self, and other on a personal and interpersonal level, Jesus also bore witness to mutual and right relationship in the social, political, and economic sphere. Jesus challenged the status quo. In a very real sense, as theological professor and author Obery M. Hendricks Jr. states in his new book, *The Politics of Jesus,* this man from Nazareth, named Jesus, was a political revolutionary, not in the usual way in which we think of a political revolutionary who is involved in politics, power games, or the forceful overthrow of a government. It does mean, however,

> that an important goal of his ministry was to radically change the distribution of authority and power, goods and resources, so all people particularly the little people, or the "least of these," as Jesus called them—might have lives free of political repression, enforced hunger and poverty, and undue insecurity. It means that Jesus sought not only to heal people's pain but also to inspire

50. Williams, *Sisters in the Wilderness,* 201.

and empower people to remove the unjust social and political structures that too often were the cause of their pain.[51]

Justice, love, and compassion formed the foundation of Jesus' ministry, which flowed from his own spirit in mutual relation with the Spirit of God. In his relationship with individuals Jesus invited them to live and breathe in this Spirit, knowing in the very ground of his being that this Spirit held the power for radical connectedness and empowerment. This Spirit was the sacred source of human life, and this power was sacred power, and Jesus sought to share it with all others in the hope that others too would experience their own source and power. As Carter Heyward states, "God's Power and Spirit are ours, as they were Jesus of Nazareth's, insofar as we are making justice-love in the world, in smaller and larger realms of our life together."[52]

This justice-love, which Jesus embodied, was not the love of eros, a romantic love. It was not the love of *philia*, the love between friends. Rather, it was agape love, a goodwill towards all men, a love that suffers and forgives, an unconditional love, a love as God loves. In our contemporary times, Martin Luther King Jr. may best reflect such love. In both words and actions, Martin Luther King Jr. lived a theology of mutual relation. He understood full well the interrelationship of the individual to God, self, and other, affirming that all human beings possess dignity and worth because in relationship to God all human beings are valued and worthwhile. This agape love that he preached and practiced was rooted in his belief that God was not an omnipotent monarch in the heavens, but rather that God was the very substance of all of life, rooted in the very fibers of our existence; and this substrate of creation, our own human creation and all the creation that surrounds us is love, for indeed, God is love. This agape love, King asserted, "is the love of God operating in the human heart."[53]

It is this divine-human relation that Jesus of Nazareth embodies and envisions, a relationship of mutuality, a relationship of care and connection, of concern and compassion, and Jesus calls out to all who will listen for actualization of this relation with God, self, and other. This mutual relation, this interdependence and interconnection with God and all of

---

51. Hendricks, *Politics of Jesus*, 5.

52. Heyward, *Saving Jesus*, 55.

53. King, "An Experiment in Love," 19.

God's creation is grounded in love. In her book, *Saving Jesus from Those Who Are Right,* Heyward states, "The story of the brother from Nazareth and his friends is about making connection among ourselves, building community for the purpose of rooting and grounding the love of God in the world around and between and within us."[54]

OUR POWER IN MUTUAL RELATION

In the mutuality of relationship, this love undergirds our life together in community, and herein lies our power. For if indeed relationship is everything, a theology of mutual relation invites us into shared power with God, and in turn, into shared power with all others. Power that is shared, however, undermines authoritarian relationships whether those relationships are with God or with others. Shared power is transformational power, and all too often we as human creatures, as well as our created structures and institutions, resist transformation. Perhaps our resistance stems from a deep, intuitive sensing and fear of what would be required, for as Carter Heyward challenges us, "We know, do we not, that if we actually go with this power in mutual relation, our lives will be changed radically. A transformation will take place at the root of who we are."[55]

Like Carter Heyward, King understood that a theology of mutual relation was not just about our interpersonal relationships but encompassed the sociopolitical realm as well. Like Walter Wink, King understood the evils inherent in the Domination System, inherent in the whole structure of society. Like Jesus, Martin Luther King embodied justice-love by challenging the status quo and bearing witness to the necessity for establishing mutual and right relationship in the very fabric of societal structures, knowing full well that "radical reconstruction of society itself is the real issue to be faced."[56]

Indeed, within a theology of mutual relation, the radical reconstruction of the present system of retributive justice with its ethos of redemptive violence and evil hegemony of authoritarian power, control, and exploitation, is required. Reconstructing the present system of retributive justice within the framework of a theology of mutual relation, within the fabric of agape love, a love as God loves, requires us to seek and find the means of transforming a system of retribution into a system of restoration.

54. Heyward, *Saving Jesus,* 111.

55. Ibid., 107.

56. King, "A Testament of Hope," 315.

Such a task is not easy; the solutions are not simple; all of it is complex and convoluted. Without a doubt, the Powers seem daunting, overwhelming, and insurmountable. The Sacred Power, however, which lies within us, among us, and between us, is greater than the task ahead of us. Surely, this shared Sacred Power enabled and empowered Martin Luther King Jr. to bring down the tenacious and towering walls of segregation. This Sacred Power, embodied in Jesus of Nazareth, allowed him to transcend the violence visited upon him, for as Walter Wink states,

> In his death he challenged the entire System of Dominance. The Powers threw at him every weapon in their arsenal. But they could not deflect him from the trail that he and God were blazing. Because he lived thus, we too can find our own path.[57]

A THEOLOGY OF MUTUAL RELATION
AS MIRRORED IN RESTORATIVE JUSTICE

This path that Jesus of Nazareth followed was grounded in a theology of mutual relation. Jesus modeled for us a way of living in right relationship with God, self, and other. It is this mutual relation, this connection and community grounded in the love of God, which offers the greatest hope of healing our deepest wounds, of restoring the brokenness of our lives, of soothing the sorrow, the suffering, the struggle of our lives, and of transforming the tragedy of our human living. It is sorely lacking in the present system of imprisonment and punishment. Indeed, at times, it is seemingly nonexistent. Instead, the present system is piloted and propelled via power relations, domination, and disconnection. For the most part, it perpetuates this evil that is its source.

Restorative justice holds its own challenges and complexities; it is not a panacea. It does, however, hold the promise and possibility of restoring right relationship among people, among all those people involved in the "crime": the victim, the offender, and the community. Restorative justice considers the needs of the crime victims; it considers the accountability of the offender, the harm he or she has inflicted as well as the harm he or she may have suffered as a result of his or her own past victimization; and it considers the impact the offense has had on the community as well as the social, economic, and political aspects within the community that may have contributed to the offense. The

57. Wink, *Engaging the Powers*, 140–41.

interrelationships of all involved are attended to and in this way offer hope for healing and shalom, for restoring right relationship to the extent possible.

In this way, restorative justice may come closest to mirroring a theology of mutual relation, for in the words of Howard Zehr,

> If I had to put restorative justice into one word, I would choose respect: respect for all, even those who are different from us, even those who seem to be our enemies. Respect reminds us of our interconnectedness but also of our differences. Respect insists that we balance concern for all parties.[58]

Concern, care, compassion, and connection are interwoven in a theology of mutual relation, and it is in this very fabric that we find our power. Carter Heyward reminds us,

> The Jesus story is about our relational power. It is a story told to cut through the illusion that we are impotent in relation to evil. The story of the brother from Nazareth and his friends is about making connection among ourselves, building community for the purpose of rooting and grounding the love of God in the world around and between and within us. That is the only response to evil that has a prayer of working.[59]

And so may our prayer be to root and ground ourselves in this Sacred Power, in the love of God, in this mutual relation, in order that we may transform ourselves and transform our world.

Such transformation, in the midst of everyday human weakness, failure, and transgression, requires a humble acknowledgement of our own shortcomings and wrongdoings that we may exercise care and compassion with the shortcomings and wrongdoings of others. Just as God is ultimately rational, reasonable, and restorative in the midst of punishment, so too we must learn how to exercise punishment in rational, reasonable, and restorative ways. Just as God always remains connected to us and continues to hold us in relationship, always ready to forgive, so too we must learn ways to remain connected to one another, to continue to hold one another in relationship, and be ready to forgive one another.

58. Zehr, *Little Book of Restorative Justice*, 36.

59. Heyward, *Saving Jesus*, 111.

QUESTIONS FOR REFLECTION AND DISCUSSION

1. What is your image of God? Consider the source of this image. What Biblical images of God are most meaningful for you? What are the characteristics of these images? Consider the many Biblical images of God: Isa 2:10; Ps 35; Ps 24:7–10; Exod 19:18; Isa 66:12–13; Prov 1:20–33; John 15:13; Mark 14:36; Luke 15:8. What image of God is most present in your church community?

2. What are your concepts of God with regard to punishment? Do you imagine God to be punitive or restorative? Authoritarian or relational? How does this influence your understanding about how you treat yourself and others? How does this influence your capacity to forgive?

3. Do you think it is possible for our images of God to influence our thinking and behavior with regard to wrongdoing and punishment? How might the creation of new images and metaphors for God foster restorative justice?

4. What are your preconceptions and prejudices surrounding those who are imprisoned? Have you considered the inequities in our socioeconomic system with regard to prisons and prisoners? How does Jesus' ministry inform or influence your relationship with prisoners, former prisoners, or a prison ministry?

5. If justice, love, and compassion formed the foundation of Jesus' ministry, which flowed from his own spirit in mutual relation with the Spirit of God, what ways might we find to nourish a relationship of mutuality with one another, whether it is with the victims, the perpetrators, or with our communities?

4

Three Vignettes: Fostering Forgiveness
in the Framework of Restorative Justice

*Forgiving is active and aware; it is recognizing the injury, owning the
pain, and reaching out to reframe, re-create, restore, reconstruct, rebuild,
reopen what can be opened.*

—DAVID AUGSBURGER, *HELPING PEOPLE FORGIVE*

WE ARE BORN IN relationship, and our life together on this earth,
rooted in our human limitations and fallibility, will inevitably
bring sorrow, transgression, pain, and conflict among us. A major task
of our journey in this life is to learn how to live together in peace and
harmony. Indeed, it is not just our well-being that is important, but at
this time in our human evolution our very existence depends on our
ability to learn this lesson, and learning how to forgive one another is
part of this task. This is not something that comes naturally or easily,
but our Christian tradition, with the person of Jesus of Nazareth as
our model, can guide us as we consider the role of forgiveness in our
practice of punishment with the understanding that "forgiveness aims
to restore us to communion with God, with one another, and with the
whole creation."[1]

FIRST VIGNETTE

An old schoolgirl friend had called. While we had grown up together as
next-door neighbors, sharing our days in close friendship throughout

1. Jones, "Forgiveness," 140.

our adolescent and high school years, as we grew older our paths had diverged, and we saw each other less and less often. Indeed, it had been several years since we had seen one another. Still, we kept in touch with Christmas cards and an occasional phone call. And although the passage of time created its own disconnection in our relationship, what we had shared in our younger years always seemed able to hold the power to renew and reweave the threads of connection between us.

In this particular telephone encounter, after spending some time catching up on one another's lives, the conversation turned towards my work in prison ministry with the Partakers College Behind Bars program in conjunction with Boston University's Prison Education Project. Her comments came quickly and curtly, "If someone raped my daughter, I most definitely would not support such a person receiving a college education. And why should someone who has committed a crime and has been imprisoned be given a college education when there are thousands of people on the outside who have never committed a crime and cannot even afford a college education?" I was somewhat taken aback by her reaction. Not only her words, but her tone held elements of retribution, revenge, and retaliation. At a loss as to how best to respond in the moment, I paused and merely replied, "Indeed, it is a very complex issue," and our conversation moved in another direction.

Clearly, my friend's words speak of retributive justice whereby under the law a person who has committed a wrong, deserves to be punished. Indeed, such a person should suffer, for through punishment and suffering the wrongdoer pays back a debt to society. Author Trudy Govier, in her book, *Forgiveness and Revenge*, notes, "It is perhaps a sign of our culture and of standard thinking about wrongdoing that we think first of punishment."[2] Surely, when one has been unjustly treated or injured, when a wrong has been committed, one seeks reparation, one hopes for some kind of compensation. However, punishment, in the form of retributive justice often allows little, if any, room for restoration, for forgiveness. Consequently, there is only further alienation among members of the human family, wider division among the community, and deeper disconnection from self, other, and in turn, from God.

2. Govier, *Forgiveness and Revenge*, 135.

RESTORATIVE JUSTICE AND FORGIVENESS

In contrast, restorative justice, seeking as it does to promote healing among all those involved—the victim, the offender, and the community—provides a completely different paradigm with regard to punishment. With its underlying foundation to make things right, restorative justice provides fertile soil from which forgiveness may take root and grow, for it fosters reconnection in and among the human community. In his book, *Helping People Forgive*, David Augsburger likens forgiveness to a bridge:

> A bridge must bear weight; forgiveness must hold up under the coming and going of life. A bridge must be connected at both ends; forgiveness must show some measure of movement from both offended and offender. A bridge must stretch, unsupported, across vast emptiness; forgiveness must risk the unknown, the unsupported, the unpredictable. A bridge must join the separated, connect the severed; forgiveness rejoins, reconnects, or constructs a new path.[3]

That the healing and restoration of people and their relationships with one another and with God was the foundation of Jesus of Nazareth's ministry, there can be little doubt. His cry from the cross, "Father, forgive them for they know not what they do," and his Sermon on the Mount, calling for love of one's enemies, serves to model for us the living out of right relationship. And it is important to remember that a calling to love one's enemies and those who have hurt us is not only a Christian notion but is one found in the major world religions, and, the notion of living in healthy relationships "necessarily implies an attitude and practice of forgiveness."[4] While it is not necessarily easy and not always completely achievable, it is, nonetheless, an attitude and practice that we can cultivate.

One means of cultivation is to foster a deeper understanding of forgiveness in the context of biblical justice. Primary in both Hebrew Scripture and the New Testament is the underlying foundation of God in relationship to God's people. From the very beginning, God's purpose is to create goodness and harmony for human beings in the living out of God's kingdom on earth. From the very beginning the human tendency

---

3. Augsburger, *Helping People Forgive*, 6–7.

4. Ellis, "Exploring the Unique Role of Forgiveness," 400.

towards disharmony and evil is evident. Yet still, from the very beginning, God seeks to remain in right relationship with humanity. While there are multiple declarations and demonstrations of God's anger and wrath, such emotion is always tempered by God's mercy and restoration of relationship with the children of the created covenant.

This covenantal relationship within the Hebrew Scriptures had as its foundational premise the concept of shalom, of right relationship, of a right way of living. Human beings were called to be in right relationship with self, with other, and with God. Whatever laws and regulations were established as part of the covenant were a means whereby God's children could remain in right relationship and live their lives accordingly. In this sense then, "justice has to do with shalom relationships and this is fundamental to what God is about, to who God is, and to what we are to be."[5]

Further, in the New Testament, the life of Jesus with his charge and challenge to love one's enemies takes the covenantal relationship to a new and deeper level. The story of the woman taken in adultery, encircled by her human brothers and sisters ready to stone her to death, may well provide the clearest and simplest lesson in the practice of forgiveness with the quiet, humble words offered by Jesus, "Let him who has not sinned be the one to cast the first stone." Jesus embodies God's loving mercy testifying to a justice rooted in care and compassion. In his article, "Retributive Justice, Restorative Justice," Howard Zehr affirms, "Jesus' primary focus is on the ethic of love and forgiveness rather than punishment."[6] Indeed, the question becomes, "If I worship a God who *never, never, never, never, never* stops loving me, what does that mean for loving the other?"[7] Jesus not only challenges us to a radical transformation of our relationships with one another, Jesus also invites us into a transformation of our relationship with God. States Zehr, "Characteristic of covenant justice, God offers forgiveness—not because we have earned it or deserve it—but because God loves us. The slate can in fact be wiped clean."[8] While with God, the slate may in fact be wiped clean, with one another, this may be more difficult. The more serious the transgression,

---

5. Zehr, *Changing Lenses*, 136.

6. Zehr, "Retributive Justice, Restorative Justice," 79.

7. Valerie Dixon, "Christian Ethics"(lecture, Andover Newton Theological School, Newton, MA, October 28, 2002).

8. Zehr, *Changing Lenses*, 157.

the greater the wound, may make it extremely difficult, if not impossible, to wipe the slate clean. However, restorative justice, with its foundation of shalom, of making things right among all those involved to the extent possible, allows for the possibility of reconnection, reconstruction, and restoration of human relationships. In this way, forgiveness allows for the possibility for all those involved to begin again, to begin anew, and in this sense the slate can be wiped clean.

Consequently then, biblical justice with its foundation of covenant and shalom, with its foundation of creating, maintaining, and restoring right relationship of human beings to self, to other, to God, stands in stark opposition to retributive justice, which so often serves only to further isolate and alienate human and divine relationship; and in isolation and alienation there is little hope for a spirit of forgiveness. In contrast, restorative justice, with its goal of making things right, may reflect biblical justice most closely. Certainly, it seeks to foster connections between people, with the principal focus on the victim rather than on the perpetrator, yet with genuine care and respect for the perpetrator and the harms they themselves have experienced, which may well be a contributing cause to his or her behavior. With its additional concern for the well-being of the larger community, restorative justice encompasses qualities of empathy, compassion, and restoration, which help to facilitate a practice of forgiveness. The Reverend David Couper, an Episcopal priest and former police chief, provides testimony to this when he states, "Restorative justice seeks healing between individuals and between people and their institutions. It is the seeking of the biblical 'shalom': inner peace, wholeness, and completeness of both individuals and their society."[9]

WE ALL STAND IN NEED OF FORGIVENESS

Cultivating a spirit of forgiveness is no easy task. Often it goes against the very grain of our human nature. It seems we are more readily programmed in the spirit of an eye for an eye. Yet, as Martin Luther King Jr. reminded us, this only leaves everyone blind. In his book, *Strength to Love*, King states, "Jesus eloquently affirmed from the cross a higher law. He knew that the old eye-for-an-eye philosophy would leave everyone blind. He did not seek to overcome evil with evil. He overcame evil with

9. Couper, "Forgiveness in the Community," 129.

good. Although crucified by hate, he responded with aggressive love."[10] This love was not aggressive in the usual sense of attacking or assaulting, but rather of advancing in a spirit of nonviolent love that encompasses the greater good with care and compassion.

Similarly, restorative justice as compared to retributive justice, allows for the possibility that all eyes may see, that relationships may be restored, that the seeds of forgiveness may take root and flourish. If our present-day, culturally accepted thinking about wrongdoing could be enlarged and transformed from one of retributive justice to one of restorative justice, whereby perpetrators would be held accountable, reparation would be sought for victims, and the larger community would be involved in rebuilding a sense of right relationships, then fostering a spirit of forgiveness might more easily be nurtured. In their essay, "Healing, Reconciliation, and Forgiving after Genocide and Other Collective Violence," authors Ervin Staub and Laurie Anne Pearlman, with regard to restorative justice, state, "Such a process requires the active involvement of the perpetrators, who are participants in rather than victims of the process, and could contribute to healing, forgiving, and reconciliation."[11]

Restorative justice, requiring as it does the involvement of perpetrators, victims, and communities, in this way acknowledges the value of persons, which in turn underlies a spirit of forgiveness. The wrong committed, the deed perpetrated, may well be deemed outrageous, monstrous, and in a certain sense, unforgivable. Yet, the individual perpetrator of the wrong is still a person, still a human being, and in Christian theology, made in the image of God. It is this truth that one hopes to respond to; it is this truth that provides the basis for hope in the possibility for human goodness and redemptive change, and in fostering forgiveness. Such a perspective, according to Govier, "means adopting and acting on the attitude that serious and resolutely unrepentant offenders are, for all their wrongdoing, persons, and persons capable of various kinds of actions of choice and change."[12] Surely, this was the attitude of Jesus as he hung on the cross between two thieves. This gospel narrative of forgiveness provides testimony that always, until the moment we draw our last breath, there is the possibility for positive choice, change, and transformation.

10. King, *Strength to Love*, 42.
11. Staub and Pearlman, "Healing, Reconciliation, and Forgiving," 220.
12. Govier, *Forgiveness and Revenge*, 137.

Allowing for such possibility would seem to require an openness of mind, heart, and spirit. Forgiveness in the context of restorative justice asks that all involved open themselves both to the pain of the injury sustained and to the ways the wounds of the injury might be healed. It requires a willingness on the part of all to seek understanding. In his book, *No Future without Forgiveness*, Desmond Tutu reminds us that forgiveness "involves trying to understand the perpetrators and so have empathy, to try to stand in their shoes and appreciate the sort of pressures and influences that might have conditioned them."[13] In contrast, retributive justice, with its goal to punish, does not seek for understanding that could help to foster empathy and forgiveness, but rather seeks justice by imposing judgment and penalty. Retributive justice, with its premise of crime being an unlawful action against the state, loses sight of people and of their relationships between and with one another. States Howard Zehr, in his book, *Doing Life*, "The actual people involved— victims and offenders—are ignored. So, too, are their experiences, their needs, and their roles."[14] Whenever our experiences and our needs are ignored, our sense of self at its deepest core feels violated. There is hurt, there is anger, there may well be shame and rage, all of which may foster greater disconnection and violence.

In bringing together perpetrator, victim, and community, restorative justice emphasizes the humanity of all, which can help to facilitate understanding and forgiveness. To one degree or another all of us, simply by virtue of being human, have both injured others and been injured ourselves. We all stand in need of forgiveness, and at the very least we all need to be willing to foster a spirit of forgiveness. In his book, *Reconciliation: Restoring Justice*, author John W. de Gruchy offers the sobering reminder that, "All of us, whether oppressors, benefactors, or victims, are caught up together in a web of human failure and fallibility."[15] Whether offering forgiveness, asking for forgiveness, or receiving forgiveness, acknowledgement of this truth helps to offset any tendencies toward judgment or self-righteousness. Rather it seeks to ground us in a genuine sense of humility, remembering, as Archbishop Desmond Tutu

---

13. Tutu, *No Future without Forgiveness*, 271.

14. Zehr, *Doing Life*, 119.

15. de Gruchy, *Reconciliation: Restoring Justice*, 191–92.

says, "It is never easy to say, 'I am sorry'; they are the hardest words to articulate in any language."[16]

To offer an apology, to acknowledge the injury to another person, to seek forgiveness is an admission of our transgression, an admission of our guilt. Our fear is that in such acknowledgement our sense of self will somehow be diminished. If one already has a poor self-image, the difficulty in acknowledging the wrongdoing may seem well-nigh impossible. In his book, *Changing Lenses*, author Howard Zehr states, "Offenders utilize a variety of defensive techniques to avoid guilt and maintain their sense of self-worth."[17] For the victim also, in offering forgiveness, there may seem to be a sense of self-diminishment, as if one is dismissing the injury, letting the perpetrator off the hook so to speak. Here too, Zehr offers an important reminder, "Forgiveness is letting go of the power the offense and the offender have over a person. Real forgiveness, then, is an act of empowerment and healing. It allows one to move from victim to survivor."[18]

In the context of retributive justice, there is little if any opportunity for the healing that can come through forgiveness. The system of meting out punishment as the sole response to a crime or injury only serves to reinforce the defenses of the perpetrator and the helplessness of the victim. The judgment and sentencing of the perpetrator, from the perspective of the judicial system, puts closure on the case. For the victim, however, it is not that simple. The array and complexity of the emotions experienced as a result of the wrongdoing may continue for months and years, and the current system of retributive justice offers no path to genuine dialogue between victim, perpetrator, and the immediate community of persons affected by the injury, which might foster understanding, empathy, and the possibility for the process of forgiveness to begin.

VIGNETTE TWO

That forgiveness is a process, which often takes place over time with a complexity of human interactions and dynamics (both personally and interpersonally, involving many psychosocial issues), can be seen in the following vignette.

---

16. Tutu, *No Future without Forgiveness*, 175.
17. Zehr, *Changing Lenses*, 49.
18. Ibid., 47.

On a gray, overcast, raw December afternoon I drove to Framingham State Prison for Women for my monthly visit to Lynne, an inmate enrolled in the Partakers College Behind Bars program in conjunction with the Boston University Prison Education Project. After parking the car, I removed my earrings and watch, gathered up my license, car registration, pen, quarters for locking up my belongings, and headed toward the front door. The dour weather mirrored the sense of despondency and depression that always seemed to sweep over me momentarily as I faced the red-brick prison edifice enclosed with barbed wire fencing and walked into the cold, uninviting visitors' lobby. I would rather not have been there; it was never a pleasant experience. The process for being cleared for visitation could easily feel intimidating and, at times even punitive.

On the other side of the steel doors Lynne was waiting for me. Greeting me with a smile and a warm hug, we were quickly engaged in conversation as she shared news of her coursework, her final exam the coming week, her expectation and excitement over receiving an A, the challenges of her job, and news of her young nieces. And for a brief time, in our human connection across many barriers, my feelings of despondency and depression amidst the prison environment dissipated. Indeed, momentarily, I forgot where I actually was.

Then, our conversation turned to my own coursework on forgiveness and reconciliation and Lynne shared from her own experience and insights. Then I remembered; yes, she was serving a sentence for second degree murder. Though unintentional, in the heat of one moment, her life had changed irrevocably. I listened as she spoke of forgiveness.

> Many prisoners are not given the chance to tell families and kids how sorry they are. The people on the outside don't know the pain or remorse many inmates feel. The forgiveness is not only around the inmates and their crime but many girls in here have to learn to forgive the people who have abused them both physically and mentally. It is mostly these acts that have resulted in involvement with drugs and crime. I had to learn to forgive other people in my life before I could begin to heal myself. People don't see the hell and pain women in here have suffered. They never learned to live with the things that have happened to them. Instead, they found their own way to deal. It is important for women in here to learn they didn't deserve the things that happened to them. Perhaps,

then, many others can see that they didn't know any other way to deal, then forgive them, and help to teach them a better way.[19]

Indeed, I acknowledged to Lynne, that out of my own experience, I could testify full well to the connection between healing and forgiveness.

HEALING AND FORGIVENESS

In his book, *The Art of Forgiveness*, theologian Geiko Muller-Fahrenholz attests, "An act of forgiveness must be understood as a complex process of 'unlocking' painful bondage, of mutual liberation. While perpetrators must be set free from their guilt (and its devastating consequences), the victims must be liberated from their hurt (and its destructive implications)."[20] Lynne's acknowledgement that she needed to forgive other people in her life before she could begin to heal herself holds wisdom and truth. Author L. William Countryman states, "What the matter comes down to, then, is that I need to forgive others for the sake of my own well-being. If I refuse to begin the process of forgiveness, I will find myself locked up in the pain of past wrongs."[21] Consequently, a system of retributive justice, which disallows for the process of forgiveness, all too often keeps both perpetrator and victim imprisoned. With its premise that an offense is a crime against the state, retributive justice fails to acknowledge the humanity of all involved and thus contributes to deepening alienation and isolation. In such a climate, healing is difficult, for as Augsburger states, "We cannot heal ourselves; healing is either actualized, mediated, or surrogated within community. We are healed by the other; we heal each other."[22]

FORGIVENESS AS PROCESS AND PRACTICE

Forgiveness is often a complex process, is not always easy, and indeed, it can be extremely painful. As L. Gregory Jones reminds us, "On paper, forgiveness is great. The problem comes when we try to take it off the page and live it out in our actual relations with one another."[23] Frequently, it involves wrestling with and working through deep and intense emotions

19. Lynne, conversation with author, March 15, 2005.
20. Muller-Fahrenholz, *Art of Forgiveness*, 25.
21. Countryman, *Forgiven and Forgiving*, 53.
22. Augsburger, *Helping People Forgive*, 97–98.
23. Jones, "Forgiveness," 134.

of anger, frustration, rage, helplessness, guilt, depression, and despair. Forgiveness does not usually happen in a moment. Almost always, it is a process, often a long, arduous process. Indeed, this cannot be emphasized enough, for as a process, it takes time, perhaps even months and years. "Forgiving is a journey; the deeper the wound, the longer the journey." [24] Whenever one has suffered a serious injury, a severe injustice, saying "I forgive you" may seem simplistic and insufficient. Yet often, the mere articulation of those few words may set one on the journey of forgiveness. Likewise, saying, "I'm sorry," may sound trite and insignificant in light of the injury sustained. Yet again, the mere articulation of those few words may open the door for forgiveness, healing, and restoration of persons to self, to others, to community, and to God. Again, the Reverend David Couper provides a most important insight: "The ability to give and to ask for forgiveness is one of the things which make us human." [25] To give and ask for forgiveness restores our humanity, it restores the ties that bind us together, and it strengthens our bonds to one another as well as our bonds in the human community.

STEPS IN FORGIVENESS

Within community we may find the strength to take steps towards forgiveness. In recent years, there has been much written about forgiveness, and different models have been set forth. One such model is offered by psychologist Robert Enright in his book, *Forgiveness Is a Choice*. The first step is to look directly at the injury, to uncover the anger and the pain of the injury. [26] This allows for the release of the true feelings and the emotional impact of the injury. In this way, both the danger of buried anger and resentment, as well as the possibility of denial and dismissal of the injury is lessened. The second step is making a decision to forgive with a willingness to begin the forgiveness process. [27] Such a decision is not easy, for it involves giving up feelings of resentment and desires for retaliation. It involves a willingness to change our thinking in regard to the one who has caused the injury. This, then, leads to the third step, which is working towards understanding and feeling compassion to-

24. Smedes, *Art of Forgiving*, 178.
25. Couper, "Forgiveness in the Community," 126.
26. Enright, *Forgiveness Is a Choice*, 78.
27. Ibid., 79.

ward the offender, acknowledging that we, too, have injured others; that we, too, stand in need of forgiveness; and that perhaps, given the deck of cards that life has dealt the offender, we, too, might have caused harm in a similar way. As Enright reminds us, "Offenders act as they do for reasons. These may not be justifiable but they may be understandable. Understanding the forces that drive offenders is an important aspect of the forgiveness process."[28] Finally, the fourth step is to reflect upon the meaning of the hurt and harm we have experienced, recognizing that we are not alone in our suffering, for suffering is part of the human condition, and this we share with all of our brothers and sisters.[29]

These steps provided in Enright's model certainly intersect in part with practices of restorative justice. Bringing together victim and perpetrator allows for the first step of naming the injury and uncovering the anger and pain of the injury. While the second step of making a decision to forgive may or may not be part of a restorative justice practice, the possibility for a change in thinking with regard to the one who has caused the injury is often an outcome of victim-offender mediation, which may in turn lead to a decision to forgive. Certainly, in the restorative justice practices of community conferencing and community peacemaking circles, there is the real opportunity for the third step. This leads to an understanding of the offender and compassion for the offender with the recognition that we are all part of the larger human family, with all of us always standing in need of forgiveness. Then in considering the fourth step as described by Enright, restorative justice practices, all of which incorporate the opportunity for addressing the injury in the presence of others and in sharing that with others in a caring and supportive environment, certainly allows for reflection on the meaning of the injury and harm experienced. As L.Gregory Jones reminds us, "Learning to live as forgiven and forgiving people is a lifelong task . . . none of us is finished with learning the practice."[30]

WHAT FORGIVENESS IS AND IS NOT

Forgiveness is a process that often takes place over months and years, and one which may never be completed. The memory of the injury, the

28. Ibid., 140.
29. Ibid., 78.
30. Jones, "Forgiveness," 145.

pain of the injury may always be there, although it may lessen in its intensity. To expect that we can forgive once and for all, to expect that forgiveness will take away the pain of the injury is to set ourselves up for further hurt, disappointment, and resentment. The willingness to begin the process of forgiveness, of taking that first step of naming the injury, of feeling the pain may well feel akin to walking into a fiery furnace, with no hope of survival. In the midst of a supportive and caring community, however, we discover that the furnace has, instead, refined us like gold. Otherwise, states Enright, "unforgiveness, bitterness, resentment, and anger are like the four walls of a prison cell. Forgiveness is the key that opens the door and lets you out of that cell."[31]

Not only is forgiveness a process, it is also a practice, and remembering what forgiveness is *not* assists us in the practice. Forgiveness is not forgetting. The old adage, "forgive and forget" is actually of no genuine value, for what is implied is the burying of the memory of the injury, a suppression of the injustice. Most often, this only serves to impede healing and forgiveness. What is necessary is an acknowledgement of the truth to oneself, to others in community, and hopefully, to the one who has caused the injury.

Forgiveness is not a demand or a command. Rather, it is a gift freely given. Indeed, this is part of its healing essence, and it may well be that this is so because inherent in the gift, acknowledged or unacknowledged, recognized or unrecognized, is some degree of humility and empathy. A genuine sense of humility helps us to remember our place in the sphere of human living. It keeps us from a false sense of pride, of self-righteousness; it keeps us from losing sight of our own human weakness and fallibility. In this way, it helps us remain connected to one another for within humility is the understanding that as a human being, I too, am capable of inflicting harm and injury on another human being. Humility helps us to foster compassion for one another. Then within empathy is the understanding, however small, of the feelings, the thoughts, the world of this other human being who has inflicted harm and injury.[32] Humility and empathy together are the soil from which a healing connection may take root and grow.

Forgiveness is not the same as reconciliation. On some level, forgiveness is always a decision followed by action, either inwardly, out-

31. Ibid., 79.

32. Worthington, "Pyramid Model of Forgiveness," 123.

wardly, or both. Forgiveness sets the stage for reuniting the offender and the one who has been harmed, but such reuniting does not necessarily have to follow forgiveness. As psychologist Everett Worthington notes, "Forgiveness happens inside an individual; reconciliation happens within a relationship."[33] Whether or not reconciliation takes place, the practice of forgiveness can, in and of itself, foster liberation and healing.

Forgiving is not passive acceptance. Passive acceptance of an injury or injustice sustained serves no constructive or creative purpose. It is a kind of denial and as such diminishes the victim's personhood. While the acknowledgement of the truth may well be difficult and painful, it can simultaneously prove liberating and empowering. Likewise, a passive acceptance diminishes the personhood of the perpetrator as well, for it does not hold that person accountable for his or her own actions. Harming another is always serious and significant. Howard Zehr points out, "It was bad, it does matter, and to deny that is to devalue both the experience of suffering and the very humanity of the person responsible."[34] Forgiveness, then, is not condoning; it is not about giving up the pain. Indeed, a deeper understanding of pain allows for forgiveness.

Understanding the pain is a mutual process for both victim and offender. Both must stand under the pain—their own pain and the pain of the other. The natural, innate human tendency is to push the pain away, to flee from it, to fight against it, to strike out both at it and at the one who has caused the pain. A professor of pastoral care and counseling, David Augsburger, in his book, *Helping People Forgive*, states, "The reflex of pain is to inflict pain."[35] Most often, however, such tendencies serve only to intensify the pain. Retributive justice, with its underlying premise of punishment as infliction of pain disallows for the absorption or the bearing of pain. Instead, the perpetrator must defend him- or herself against the pain of guilt, the pain of punishment. Such defenses impede the process of forgiveness. Restorative justice, on the other hand, which promotes dialogue between the offender and the victim and which gives the offender a role in the solution and responsibility for a resolution to the injury, allows for the acknowledgement of the pain inflicted and also for the pain in the offender's life that may have contributed to the harm inflicted. And simultaneously, with the victim's needs being central, re-

33. Ibid., 129.

34. Zehr, *Changing Lenses*, 46–47.

35. Augsburger, *Helping People Forgive*, 154.

storative justice provides a forum for the victim's suffering and pain to be expressed and to be heard, a necessary step in the process of forgiveness. In contrast, in the system of retributive justice, the victim's pain and suffering most often gets lost amidst the drama of the courts and the focus on the establishment of guilt and punishment of the offender.

Acknowledging the pain, absorbing the pain, and bearing the pain takes courage, and we need all the help we can get. Herein lies the importance of community, and the restorative justice model—with its involvement of the larger community of family, friends, neighbors in seeking understanding, healing, and reparation of the injury inflicted—provides the opportunity for both victim and perpetrator to acknowledge the pain, bear up under the pain, and walk through the pain. Surely, this was the model offered in South Africa under the Truth and Reconciliation Commission. While far from perfect, it provided an alternative, an alternative witnessed worldwide, to the usual reaction to simply inflict more pain in retaliation for pain incurred. Psychologist, Pumla Gobodo-Madikizela, who served with Archbishop Desmond Tutu on the Human Rights Violations Committee of South Africa's Truth and Reconciliation Commission states, "The Truth and Reconciliation Commission was a strategy not only for breaking the cycle of politically motivated violence but also for teaching important lessons about how the human spirit can prevail even as victims remember the cruelty visited upon them in the past."[36] Upheld by the larger community, individuals could remember their pain and move through that pain towards healing and forgiveness.

At the heart of the Truth and Reconciliation Commission is the concept of *ubuntu*. While according to Archbishop Desmond Tutu, *ubuntu* is a difficult concept to explain in Western language, it can best be understood by the acknowledgement and affirmation that one's humanity is unquestionably interwoven with the humanity of another. One's essence as a human being is held in respect and esteem through belonging, participating, and sharing. There is the knowledge that one "belongs in a greater whole and is diminished when others are humiliated or diminished, when others are tortured or oppressed, or treated as if they were less than who they are."[37]

Restorative justice, like South Africa's Truth and Reconciliation Commission, is not perfect, but like the commission it offers the pos-

36. Gobodo-Madikizela, *A Human Being Died*, 103.
37. Tutu, *No Future without Forgiveness*, 31.

sibility for a new way, a better way through the honoring of human relationships in the context of community. In this sense, there may be an even deeper lesson to be learned from the South African experience when considering the choice for forgiveness or for retribution in the context of *ubuntu*.

VIGNETTE THREE

Ubuntu then, provides a foundation for forgiveness, for healing, for restoration. In offering a final vignette, it would seem that this was what Good Geoff discovered in the context of a weekend, in-prison workshop called the Alternatives to Violence Program. A young, African American male, already imprisoned for more than a few years, he expressed his apprehension on being released. Acknowledging to the group that he had no experience of affirmation, of goodness, of healing and hope, he spoke instead of what he did know. Growing up in the inner-city housing projects where poverty, lack of education and opportunity breed crime and violence, Good Geoff was involved with gangs, drug-dealings, and street shootings. Having witnessed his father's stabbing, he recalled his anger and his outraged cursing of his father for his tears and helplessness as he lay dying in that moment. One was expected never to cry, to always be tough. It seemed to him there was little, if any, hope for a different kind of life. Nevertheless, at the close of the weekend, having participated in a variety of experiences helping to foster trust, affirmation, and community building, the group of inmates and outside facilitators joined in a circle, and as each one acknowledged what he or she had learned from the weekend, Good Geoff declared, "I've learned there's another world out there."

The realization and the experience of our shared humanity across the many barriers that separate us may be a key ingredient towards a spirit of forgiveness and healing in the brokenness of our human relationships. As L. William Countryman points out, "Different as we are from one another, vast as the gap is between the most saintly of saints, and the most vicious of genocidal demagogues, we are still more like one another than we are like anyone or anything else in this universe. And our most fundamental likeness is our ongoing ability to change and to grow and to respond to love."[38] Recognition of this fundamental likeness

---

38. Countryman, *Forgiven and Forgiving*, 64.

softens our hearts, helps to counteract our tendency towards judgment of others and self-righteous attitudes. It assists in promoting a spirit of forgiveness.

In remembering our shared humanity we remember that our life here on earth exists in relationship to and with one another. Restorative justice fosters right relationship. In doing so, it counters the prevailing notion that criminal activity is an action against the state. Rather, it serves to underscore the truth, which is that criminal activity is unjust activity that takes place between people. And it is the relationships between people that must be healed and restored.

Restorative justice as a growing movement may provide not only a practical framework for fostering a spirit of forgiveness but also a genuine means of transforming attitudes and practices towards facilitating a spirit of forgiveness. Restorative justice can help us to remember that "the real story of the Bible from the Old Testament into the New is this: God does not give up. It is precisely in this way that we are to imitate God, to be 'perfect': in indiscriminate love, in love that is undeserved, in forgiveness, in mercy."[39]

Of key importance and necessity is the fostering of a conscious awareness and remembrance of our human condition, that we have all sinned and been sinned against, that always we stand in need of forgiveness and always we need to be ready to forgive. Whether victim or perpetrator, it is necessary, indeed imperative, that we recognize, as author Trudy Govier states, "Our multiple affiliations provide grounds for pride and shame, innocence and complicity, suffering and acting, forgiveness and acknowledgement. We are both sinned against and sinners."[40] Whether victim or perpetrator, to deny ourselves the process of forgiveness, individually or collectively, is to deny ourselves individually and collectively of the hope of rebirth and renewal in our human journey towards transforming ourselves and participating in the creation of God's kingdom here on earth, in the creation of the beloved community.

---

39. Zehr, *Changing Lenses*, 146.
40. Govier, *Forgiveness and Revenge*, 156.

QUESTIONS FOR REFLECTION AND DISCUSSION

1. Which one of the three vignettes speaks to you? Who do you most identify with?

2. Are there people or certain acts that you feel are unforgivable? Do you feel there are limits to forgiveness? How do you understand your feelings or beliefs in relation to your own experiences?

3. What helps us see the perpetrator of a wrong as a person, a human being made in the image of God, and in need of forgiveness? Reflect on the words of Jesus in Luke 23:39–43.

4. Reflect on the words of Archbishop Desmund Tutu p. 73. What makes it so hard to say the words, "I'm sorry"? Can you speak to this out of your own experience?

5. Describe a time when you have offered forgiveness, or received forgiveness, and experienced healing.

5

Healing and Connection
through Compassionate Witnessing

Whatever God does, the first outburst is always compassion.

—MEISTER ECKHART, *PEACEMAKING DAY BY DAY*

HEALING AND CONNECTION ARE undoubtedly nurtured through forgiveness. Healing and connection are also nourished through compassionate witnessing. Whether or not we are aware of it, with eyes to see and ears to hear, we are always witnesses. Often our witnessing is unintentional and often we are unaware in our role as witnesses. Compassionate witnessing calls us to aware and intentional witnessing. In her book, *Common Shock*, Kaethe Weingarten states, "Each of us has opportunities in our daily life to practice intentional witnessing, where we can assist others and avoid feeling helpless and overwhelmed ourselves. I call this compassionate witnessing."[1] Through Kaethe Weingarten's work as an associate professor of clinical psychology at Harvard Medical School and her sponsorship of the Witnessing Project at the Family Institute of Cambridge, a paradigm for witnessing has been created. Through her paradigm, Weingarten invites us into aware and active witnessing—the kind of witnessing that allows us to remain connected to one another and to remember our common humanity. From this connection and remembering, we find the courage and strength to act compassionately, whether it is in smaller or larger ways. Amidst the complexity, the challenges, and,

---

1. Weingarten, *Common Shock*, 22.

so often, the heartache of prison ministry, aware and compassionate witnessing allows us to endure and gives us hope.

CONNECTION AS PREREQUISITE FOR COMPASSIONATE WITNESSING

Fostering awareness and empowerment in prison ministry must necessarily include the basic tenet that whether one considers the perpetrator of a crime or violation, or the victim of a crime or violation, all of us are inextricably connected to both by virtue of our being connected within the human community. It would seem that recognizing this truth is a prerequisite for compassionate witnessing. Recognizing another truth, however, is equally essential: it is a natural, human impulse to disassociate, downplay, and deny the distress of others as a means of protection against our own psychological distress. Yet, our ability to hold both truths in hand simultaneously enhances our effectiveness in the area of prison ministry, for irregardless of either truth, as psychologist Kaethe Weingarten states, "We are all always witnesses."[2]

As witnesses, all of us then, to one degree or another, and in one form or another, are ceaselessly and continuously observing, attending to, surveying, supporting, authenticating, and acknowledging the world around us and those within our world. In the world of prison ministry the challenge is to keep the whole constellation in view, encompassing the experience of perpetrator, victim, community, and the criminal justice system itself. This is no easy task and one that we are not in the habit of engaging. It is, therefore, understandable that we would feel unequal to such a task, and yet in the context of Christian witnessing it seems vital to the healing and transformation of ourselves and of our world.

ALWAYS WE ARE WITNESSES

In any act of violation or violence there are three roles: perpetrator, victim, and witness. The individuals or groups who stand in these roles may or may not interact directly with one another, may or may not be visible to one another, but there is nevertheless a relationship between them. A perpetrator may never meet the victim whose house has been vandalized and may never be apprehended by the police who have been called to the scene and who bear witness to the violation, as does the neighbor

---

2. Weingarten, "Witnessing, Wonder, and Hope," 392.

who visits to offer support and consolation. Yet the victim is now witness to the disarray and destruction of his or her property, the police and neighbor, representing as they do both the criminal justice system and the community, cannot help but feel a sense of victimization even as they stand in witness. As for the perpetrator, in all likelihood that person has suffered victimization, for in most instances the perpetrator of violence and violation has suffered the very same in his or her own life. Indeed, in the most extreme cases of violence, as psychiatrist James Gilligan testifies, speaking out of his own experience working with some of the most violent prisoners, "one cannot fail to see that the men who occupy the extreme end of the continuum of violent behavior in adulthood occupied an equally extreme end of the spectrum of violent child abuse earlier in life."[3]

There is then, not only a relationship between the individuals in these roles, but the roles themselves interchange amidst the relationships of these very same individuals. In considering these roles and relationships with regard to violence and violation it may seem at first that we are examining a phenomenon outside of ourselves. However, as Kaethe Weingarten reminds us,

> The three-role drama, in which victim, perpetrator, and witness are intricately related to one another, also plays out as a drama inside every one of us. We have the potential to occupy all three roles and we all *have* acted from each role. We may not like to face this about ourselves, but most of us know this is true. It is part of the human condition.[4]

Such recognition allows for growth in awareness as we seek to create effective prison ministries in our congregations that are able to engage in compassionate witnessing.

AWARENESS AND COMPASSIONATE WITNESSING

Growing in awareness becomes essential for compassionate witnessing, the kind of witnessing that promotes healing and connection across all boundaries of relationships and roles. Beginning with self-awareness, not only is our understanding of ourselves enhanced, but also our understanding of others is facilitated as we consider ourselves in the roles of

3. Gilligan, *Violence*, 45.
4. Weingarten, *Common Shock*, 25.

victim, perpetrator, and witness. In this way, we become more effective witnesses. Awareness, however, whether it is of self or other, is always in a state of flux just by virtue of the complex demands of our daily living that make it impossible to maintain complete awareness all of the time. Nonetheless, it is important that we not allow this to serve as an excuse, for as Kaethe Weingarten reminds us, "The temptation for most of us is to remain unaware. It wards off the pain of feeling helpless or confronting our uncertainty of what to do."[5]

It may well be a truth that a lot of us remain unaware a lot of the time until such time, perhaps, that our own growth in awareness is fostered either alone or in conjunction with others. I am reminded of a time many years ago when as an adolescent I lived in a town where there was a state correctional facility. It was on the other side of town, an area that I seldom frequented, and while I was aware of its location and its purpose for housing prisoners, at that time in my young life I gave it little thought. If by chance the subject of its location arose, I was certainly aware that its presence in our community cast an invisible shadow over our lives, and even those classmates of mine who lived on the other side of town seemed to the rest of us discredited simply by their proximity to the prison facility. Did I consider the world of the prison, its history, its meaning, its purpose? Not in the least. Did I reflect on the world of the prisoner, his life, his crime, the victim of his crime? Not at all.

Several years later, having previously left the community for education and work, I returned there to live and raise my children. Now, I lived on the other side of town, indeed just a few miles up the road and around the corner from the prison. It no longer seemed so far removed from my awareness as several times a week on my way to work I would drive by its high concrete walls, with barbed wire fencing reaching up even higher, catching glimpses of the guards sealed away in their turreted towers overlooking the prison complex. For the most part, only a vague awareness stirred within me, a sense of discomfort, sadness, and isolation, and on occasion thoughts of those men inside the prison, imagining if only fleetingly, what life must be like for them.

By now, on Sundays I was attending a Quaker meeting for worship. One member was actively engaged in prison ministry leading Alternatives to Violence (AVP) workshops; another member's son who suffered from mental illness was incarcerated, and she and I became

5. Ibid., 34.

close friends; and over the next several years a community-based prison outreach group became actively involved in the life of the prison. While I was aware of a small leaning within myself towards these concerns, I remained personally removed, busy with work and raising children, and preoccupied with my own life. Essentially, to a large degree, I remained an unaware witness.

A VISUAL TOOL FOR WITNESSING IN PRISON MINISTRY

In her work on silence, voice, and witnessing, Kaethe Weingarten has created a visual tool that proves to be extremely helpful in understanding how our awareness or unawareness interfaces with empowerment or disempowerment and how that interfacing impacts our thinking, our behavior, and our ability to act or not to act. Her graphic illustration of witness positions (see below) "shows that one's position as witness is influenced by whether or not one is aware and whether or not one feels empowered in relation to any aspect of what one is witnessing."[6]

	Aware	Unaware
Empowered	1	2
Disempowered	4	3

6. Ibid., 27.

To illustrate this within the prison institution, one could use the example of a prison guard who may well be unaware of the many complexities that are part of the system under which he or she is employed, but because he or she is in a position of power, he or she would occupy the space of unaware and empowered (2). If this same person were to have the occasion or opportunity to grow in awareness in this regard, the person would move into an empowered and aware state (1). Very often, the prisoners themselves, because of their unique experience with the prison system, or because of their taking the time to educate themselves around the issues they face while imprisoned are very much aware, but because of their very imprisonment, they remain disempowered (4). So, too, many of us through our involvement in prison ministry grow in awareness but feel disempowered to effect any significant change in the system itself. In that way, we remain aware but disempowered. On the other hand, perhaps in our growing awareness we may have the opportunity to effect change within one particular prisoner, and then, in that moment we move to a position of awareness and empowerment, to a place of compassionate witnessing. It is important to remember that our growing in awareness, even though there may be no way to take action, is essential and significant, for as Weingarten reminds us, "It plants a seed. Awareness without action is neither irrelevant nor self-indulgent; it may be all that is called for at that particular moment."[7] It is important to note that one's position as witness is not static. It is possible to simultaneously occupy more than one position in relation to others involved in the process of witnessing and of course, one's position can change over time as my own continued to do.

GROWING IN AWARENESS AND WITNESSING

It would be many years later, when my children were grown and I had returned to graduate school, when the occasion for new growth in awareness and witnessing in prison ministry presented itself. By this time, I had moved from a wealthy suburb into the inner city where I was working. As a community health nurse, the patients I visited were primarily African American, as was the congregation of the church where I now worshipped. It was here that I began an internship in urban ministry as

7. Ibid., 34.

part of my graduate studies and at the suggestion of the associate minister found myself working with the church prison ministry.

A primary focus of the prison ministry that year was "Angel Tree," one aspect of Prison Fellowship, a national and international prison ministry group that partners with churches seeking to minister to prisoners, ex-prisoners, and their families. Prison Fellowship was founded by Chuck Colson after his own experience of imprisonment resulting from his involvement in the Watergate scandal during the Nixon presidency. A born-again Christian, Colson came to believe that restorative change comes to individuals and communities only through a relationship with Jesus Christ, and this formed the foundation of his prison ministry. Angel Tree was a means whereby churches could provide Christmas gifts for children of prisoners, providing opportunities to minister to both the children and their families. While I was not at all certain that restorative change comes to individuals and communities *only* through a relationship with Jesus Christ, I nevertheless immersed myself in the Angel Tree event. As I did so, my awareness as witness took on a new dimension. A few of the families that came to the church for the Angel Tree Christmas celebration, I recognized. They were the sons, daughters, grandchildren of patients whom I encountered in my nursing visits in this ghetto community. I began to see, even if only through a glass darkly, the connections between poverty, race, lack of education, lack of opportunity, and imprisonment. It would be still several years later that I would learn the facts, which Jeffrey Reiman clearly states:

> Our prisoners are not a cross section of America. They are considerably poorer and considerably less likely to be employed than the rest of Americans. Moreover, they are also less educated, which is to say less in possession of the means to improve their sorry situation.[8]

He also reminds us that "first and foremost, black Americans are disproportionately poor."[9]

Issues of race and class continued to be more apparent as I continued to grow in awareness. Witnessing in prison ministry took on new aspects. Now for the first time, I was entering into the prison environment keenly aware of the power of the institution, the power held by those

---

8. Reiman, *Rich Get Richer*, 144.

9. Ibid., 112.

who worked in the facility, both the correctional officers themselves as well as the auxiliary prison staff. Indeed, the Catholic chaplain I was working with was employed by the prison and simply by virtue of my association with him, I sensed my own place to be in a position of power. Using Robin Casarjian's book, *Houses of Healing*, we facilitated workshops around issues of anger, shame, guilt, forgiveness of self and others for groups of the incarcerated men who were mostly men of color and came from the same neighborhoods I worked in. It goes without saying that the prisoners in the workshop were in a place of disempowerment, yet over several weeks as they grew in some measure of self-awareness one could sense that they gained a certain level of empowerment even as they remained disempowered. The opportunity to connect with others in a setting that provided for empathic listening, to share experiences and feelings, to receive understanding and affirmation, provided for a shift in their witnessing position.

Undoubtedly, while completing my internship I had grown in awareness and in my capacity to witness in the area of prison ministry. For the most part, however, to a very large degree, I remained unaware, unaware of so many of the issues and dynamics involved. Now, several more years later, I can recognize the importance of awareness with regard to one's effectiveness as witness.

In the fall of 2003, I began coursework for doctoral studies, incorporating yet another internship in prison ministry. This time, I worked with Partakers, a faith-based prison ministry whose primary focus was on supporting prisoners, intellectually, emotionally, and spiritually as they sought to complete their college education under the umbrella of the Boston University Prison Education Project. My task was to mentor a young woman who had been sentenced to life imprisonment. Initially, I knew little about her. Indeed, there was concern expressed by my internship supervisor as to whether or not Lynne would even be able to complete the three prerequisite courses, for her behavior was known to be volatile and Lynne had been in and out of "the hole," a place of solitary confinement for prisoners whose behavior was in any way disruptive to the prison system.

DEEPENING GROWTH IN AWARENESS AND WITNESSING

Visiting Lynne every three to four weeks, my role as witness broadened and deepened. My position as a graduate theology student was of no significance whatsoever in the eyes of the prison administration. As a matter of fact, in their eyes I was simply another visitor, waiting in the cold, impersonal lobby with all the other visitors of inmates, waiting patiently, sometimes for nearly two hours before we were allowed to walk through the security "trap" to enter the visiting room. Experientially, I came to know the truth of Kaethe Weingarten's words, "Witnesses struggle not only with what they have seen but also with how to render to others what they have seen."[10] In prison ministry, this struggle is critical if we are to share the truth of our experiences, "for the purpose of turning private pain into public purpose."[11]

Seeing, hearing, feeling; wanting to see, hear, and feel, and yet I also knew it was essential not to be overwhelmed by these sense perceptions. Seeing the military-type uniforms of the correctional officers and watching their swagger, listening to the bark of their orders echoing back from the vaulted ceilings, feeling their own sense of power simply by virtue of this uniform they wore, it was difficult not to feel disempowered. Seeing an older visitor, a man who had driven three hours to visit his daughter whom he had not seen in months, turned away because he was not wearing the "right" kind of clothing, hearing his outburst of angry cursing as he slammed out the lobby doors, I felt the intensity of his disempowerment even as I felt disempowered with him. Seeing the children coming to visit their mothers, listening as one young girl asked her mother, "Why do they call you inmates?" and hearing her mother's vague, indirect answer, I could not help but feel the confusion and sorrow of this child's unaware disempowerment.

Now, more aware myself, knowing that in recent years the number of women prisoners has skyrocketed, knowing that "incarcerated women bear a double burden of punishment: their children 'do time' along with them, because most imprisoned women are single parents" and that "eighty percent of women in prison are mothers, and two-thirds have children under 18"[12] may have facilitated my awareness as a witness but did little to facilitate a sense of empowerment. There was, however, my growing relationship with Lynne. She was herself an incarcerated mother, having been sentenced to prison when her only daughter was ten years old. Her daughter had already been living with a foster fam-

10. Weingarten, "Witnessing, Wonder, and Hope," 393.

11. Ibid., 395.

12. Magnani and Wray, *Beyond Prisons*, 116.

ily. As chance had it, Lynne had indirect knowledge of this family because they had known her brother while growing up. When the family asked to adopt her daughter, Lynne, after careful consideration, agreed because she believed her daughter's best interest would be served by the stability of remaining in one family setting. What had seemed wise initially proved to be painful and alienating, for as the months passed the adoptive father forbid Lynne's daughter to visit. At first, the adoptive mother acted as liaison for secret written communication between Lynne and her daughter, but eventually this connection too was lost. Those moments when Lynne shared her heartache, her anger, and her helplessness, her own disempowerment with this situation, it seemed all I could do was to listen with as much empathic understanding as I could engender. I, too, felt disempowered to change the situation, but as Kaethe Weingarten notes, "In some instances awareness may be all that we can offer. Awareness without action is neither irrelevant nor self-indulgent; it may be all that is called for at that particular moment . . . awareness builds the platform for action."[13]

PRAYER AND COMPASSIONATE WITNESSING

Certainly, my awareness continued to deepen, and in a real way my monthly visits to Lynne and the ongoing support I offered as she began to move through her college courses comprised in some small way a platform of action. Nevertheless, in the face of the structural violence and violation of the prison institution, amidst the disconnection and dehumanization inherent in the system, it was difficult, to say the least, not to feel insignificant, helpless, and disempowered. Noting the importance of finding ways to overcome such feelings, Kaethe Weingarten acknowledges, "Selecting a witnessing focus is a process that begins to shift our sense of passivity and helplessness, disempowerment and numbness, into (more of) a sense of effectiveness and competence."[14]

While it seemed I did have a witnessing focus, it seemed also that I needed to seek a way to engage that process still further. I considered Walter Wink's concept of the spirituality of institutions, the need for confrontation, and the necessity of prayer. His chapter titled, "Prayer and the Powers," had always intrigued me, and I had returned to it many

13. Weingarten, *Common Shock*, 34.
14. Ibid., 193.

times. Here, he states, "the act of praying is itself one of the indispensable means by which we engage the Powers."[15] While I always entered into visitation in a spirit of prayer, I began to intentionally incorporate centering prayer into my times of visitation within the prison organization. Immediately prior to visiting I set aside a time of ten minutes for *lectio divina*,[16] a reading of Scripture that would help to provide a foundation for the following twenty minutes of centering prayer. Allowing God's presence and action to enter within allows for the possibility to discover God's presence everywhere, within all others, and within the Powers of the prison organization.

In choosing a sacred word for this time of centering prayer, the word that came to me was "Namaste." This word seemed to have a rightness to it, particularly fitting for the prison organization and my encounters with the correctional officers as I entered the brick, steel fortresses of the prison facilities. Indeed, I would say this word later, silently in my heart, as I met face to face with these individuals.

> Namaste . . . I honor the place in you where the entire universe resides: I honor the place in you of love, of light, of truth, of peace. I honor the place within you where if you are in that place in you and I am in that place in me, there is only one of us . . . Namaste.[17]

Allowing God's presence to enter within in such a way helps me to remember that God is already praying within me; it helps me to listen to the prayer already being prayed within me. Wink's reminder is helpful, "When we pray, we are not sending a letter to a celestial White House where it is sorted among piles of others. We are engaged rather in an act of co-creation, in which one little sector of the universe rises up and becomes translucent, incandescent, a vibratory center of power that radiates the power of the universe."[18]

In my more intentional witnessing, in my initial preparation for the practice of centering prayer, using a time of *lectio divina* prior to my prison visitation, I focused on scriptural passages related to prayer

---

15. Wink, *Engaging the Powers*, 297.

16. de Waal, *Seeking God*, 146–47. *Lectio divina*, practiced in the Rule of St. Benedict, is a form of reading of Scripture, in which a person reflects on a particular passage slowly and attentively and takes time to savor its essence.

17. Pax Christi USA, *Peacemaking Day by Day*, 20.

18. Wink, *Engaging the Powers*, 303.

found in Ps 6:9 "the Lord has heard my supplication; the Lord accepts my prayer"; in Mark 11:24 "so I tell you, whatever you ask for in prayer, believe that you have received it, and it will be yours"; and in Rom 12:12 "rejoice in hope, be patient in suffering, persevere in prayer."

That afternoon as I entered the waiting room of Framingham State prison, I was aware of my immediate sense of heartache, of grieving for all the women contained behind the steel and concrete walls of this prison facility. I could feel the coldness, the harshness, the indifference to humanity. The spirituality of the Powers here is all too readily palpable. I closed my eyes, took some deep breaths before walking over to find a seat in the waiting area. A few people were already seated. I recognized one woman from a previous visit; I knew she was visiting her daughter. Our eyes met, I smiled, and we exchanged greetings. It seemed to me that each such encounter allows for a breath of human warmth and connection. Inwardly, I returned to prayer, aware that the spirit of answering to that of God in every person held its own power in answering the diseased spirituality of the prison institution.

I sat down to complete my own visitation registration form and then settled into silent waiting, watching as others came in. One man in his forties, visiting for the first time, needed help with the registration form, and I offered some assistance. A fellow with a toddler arrived, and we greeted one another, picking up threads of an earlier conversation we had had. Soon, a different ambience could be felt in the room as visitors were smiling, talking with one another and the goodness of human, healing connections was present.

Then one young man needed a change of bills to purchase a snack card to take inside to the visiting area so that he could buy drinks and chips for the prisoner whom he had come to see, and he asked aloud if anyone had the necessary change. I reached into my pocket to get a second quarter to reopen my locker. While I did not have the exact change of bills, I did have the correct bill he required for the machine. In that moment, the change did not seem important, rather only the giving, the reaching out in support and caring. He offered to take my name and address so he could mail me the change he owed. While I did give him the information, I knew it did not matter if he ever mailed it to me, for by this time a sense of the flowing of the Spirit could be felt among us, a spirit among us all of sharing, of concern for one another, of human kindness. There was now a sense of empowerment here among this small group of visitors, and somehow this sense in its own way engaged the afflicted, tainted spirituality of the prison institution.

Then, however, as I was called forward with two other women by a female correctional officer who would process us through the security anteroom known as "the trap," I could quickly feel the harsh, brittle coldness reflected in her person, in her stance, in her appearance. I began to pray, silently repeating my sacred word, "Namaste" as we entered, removed our shoes, and followed her orders. As the first two women cleared, I waited, trying to keep centered in the Spirit, open and gentle, looking for a softening, an opening, however small, within her person where the love, the light, the truth, the peace of both our spirits might meet. As she cleared me through, nothing seemed to be forthcoming until she asked me to sign the security log. Then, for one fleeting moment, the faintest smile appeared on her face and the healing connection was present. My own spirit lifted as I offered gratitude and praise. Wink reminds us that the prayer needful in encountering the Powers is, "not a religious practice externally imposed, but an existential struggle against the 'impossible,' against an antihuman collective atmosphere: against images of worth and value that stunt and wither full human life."[19] Distancing, dehumanization, and disconnection are elements often experienced in encountering the Powers. Wink's reminder of the necessity of prayer can help facilitate compassionate witnessing, for prayer keeps our hearts open, and an open heart, as Weingarten states, "is absolutely essential for aware and active listening."[20]

THE DISCOMFORT OF COMPASSIONATE WITNESSING

Witnessing in a spirit of awareness and compassion allows for a greater sense of empowerment even if our witnessing results in only small changes in ourselves, others, and the world around us. In the world of prison ministry, awareness almost always entails discomfort, and compassion entails pain. Indeed, the root of the word *compassion* means "to suffer with." In writing about compassion, theologian Henri Nouwen and educators Donald McNeill and Douglas Morrison acknowledge that

> compassion asks us to go where it hurts, to enter into places of pain, to share in brokenness, fear, confusion, and anguish.

19. Ibid., 298.
20. Weingarten, *Common Shock*, 170.

> Compassion challenges us to cry out with those in misery, to
> mourn with those who are lonely, to weep with those in tears.
> Compassion requires us to be weak with the weak, vulnerable with
> the vulnerable, and powerless with the powerless. Compassion
> means full immersion in the condition of being human.[21]

Being an aware, compassionate witness in relation to the victim, the perpetrator, our communities, and those who facilitate the prison institution requires a willingness to go where it hurts, to feel the pain of the other, to feel the tragedy of our human living. Such a willingness allows us to more easily recognize and acknowledge our shared humanity, which in turn gives us strength, hope, and the opportunity for healing ourselves and our world. Together we can learn compassionate witnessing, we can become skilled in compassionate witnessing, and we can gain strength in compassionate witnessing.

Witnessing in the context of prison ministry is not an easy undertaking; it requires a willingness to step out of our comfort zones, to stretch not only our hearts and spirits, but our minds as well. Noted writer and teacher in the area of criminal and restorative justice, Howard Zehr, acknowledges his own reluctance and resistance to extend his thinking. He recalls that for years he was primarily concerned with offenders, knew very few victims, and indeed did not want to know them, believing that the emotions that would be stirred up would make it difficult for him to pursue his work as an advocate for offenders. He believed that justice for offenders need not involve victims. However, as his professional journey led him into victim-offender mediation and reconciliation programs, indeed, as he helped establish the first program in the nation, he found himself face to face with victims. He states, "As I began to listen to their voices, to hear them express their needs and perspectives, my assumptions about justice began to reel."[22] Here then is a witness, previously aware and empowered in one important dimension, and yet unaware and disempowered in another equally important, if not more important, dimension. For someone so skilled and knowledgeable as Zehr to acknowledge his limitations and liabilities after years of research and work in this area serves to underscore both the complexity of the subject and the tremendous lack of knowledge on the part of most people, including myself.

---

21. McNeill et al., *Compassion*, 4.
22. Zehr, *Transcending*, 195.

As for my own journey of witnessing in the area of prison ministry, I would have to say, that like Zehr, my focus has been turned toward the offender and the outrageous inequities of the retributive criminal justice system. Indeed, I believe it would be accurate to say that most congregational prison ministries have focused their work in a similar way. Only recently, however, has my own work of research and writing in this area led me, like Zehr, to a new level of awareness and understanding with regard to victims, violation, and violence. Unlike Zehr, who has never been the victim of serious crime, I myself *have* been the victim of serious violation and violence, and it may be this fact that deeply impacted me as I read through Zehr's presentation of portraits and stories of victims of violent crime. This, in conjunction with reading the work of Harvard professor and former prison psychiatrist, James Gilligan, in his studies of violence as a national epidemic and its roots in the very structures of our culture and society, has led me to conclude that it is imperative that we begin to educate ourselves so that we can grow in awareness, and can indeed become empowered as we seek to create effective congregational prison ministries. We need eyes to see, ears to hear, and a mind and heart to understand the whole, not just bits and pieces; and we need one another's help because we are all in this together—victims, perpetrators, and witnesses.

Howard Zehr proposes that "real justice requires that we start with victims. We need to hear these voices if we are to have a real dialogue about crime and justice. We need to hear these voices if we are to do justice."[23] If indeed we start here, it becomes impossible not to see the violence that permeates our human living on this earth, the violence that is so deeply embedded in our culture and in our consciousness. The psychology of shame and humiliation, the moral ethics of honor and shame, the inequities of class and race, the disparities of gender relations are all intertwined, deeply complex roots underlying the surface of our human relations. Indeed, if we are to be compassionate witnesses in our congregational prison ministries, we must first have some understanding, even if only a beginning understanding, of these critical dynamics, however remote they might seem, and however disturbing they might be to our ordinary worldview.

If, as compassionate witnesses, we begin with the victims and we give ear to their voices, we cannot help to feel overwhelmed, as they

23. Ibid., 196–97.

themselves do, with an array of feelings. As narrators, their stories can easily generate within us the listeners feelings of anger, rage, helplessness, pain, and a sense of shame and humiliation that seem to be a natural outcome of violation. For whenever we feel violated, even in a small way, in a seemingly insignificant way, we feel bad within ourselves; it as if we ourselves are bad. For example, the rather common experience of being the recipient of another motorist's anger, cursing, and obscene gesturing can quickly generate feelings of shame and humiliation. While many factors influence how we respond in that moment, the phenomenon of "road rage" may well be indicative of the depth of felt shame and humiliation and the need to restore honor.

This need to restore honor in the face of shame and humiliation, is according to James Gilligan, as old as civilization itself, is deeply embedded in the patriarchal structure of our society, and is the very source of the violence permeating our lives. States Gilligan, "the increased propensity toward violence that civilization has brought with it is inextricably tied to its patriarchal structure in which men and women are each assigned radically different social roles, each of which is governed by a code of honor in terms of which the members of each sex are accorded honor or dishonor, pride or shame, depending on whether of not they behave according to the moral obligations of their code."[24] Patriarchal structure of society is not only linked to gender differences, but equally important for our understanding of violence and of crime and punishment, it is also linked to class differences.

If we pause and allow ourselves to consider this fact, it should come as no surprise that the ruling class in America is both white and male. This group, although small in comparison to the remainder of society, holds in *their* hands the political and economic power, which is, in turn, responsible for the social inequalities that foster crime and violence. Indeed, when one begins to consider the social policies and laws that this small group promotes and enforces, such as the drug laws, the tax laws, criminal laws, gun laws, and policies affecting media advertising and education, it is all too easy to see that this group has a vested interest in maintaining a high rate of crime and punishment. For it is through such policies that their patriarchal power is maintained, and as Gilligan notes,

24. Gilligan, *Violence*, 267.

> We will have attained what we see all around us in America to-
> day—a society characterized by three complementary and mutu-
> ally reinforcing characteristics: 1) the richest and most powerful,
> secure, and invulnerable class in the world; 2) a middle class in
> collusion with the upper class, yet itself exploited by the latter;
> and 3) an underclass that commits a higher degree of violence
> than exists in any other developed nation on earth, with violence
> committed primarily by the poor against the poor.[25]

Truly, as we begin to seriously study these dynamics, it becomes
impossible to deny their reality; it becomes impossible to deny the relationship between structural violence and behavioral violence. They are
both sides of the same coin; they mirror one another. When one begins
to study the dynamics of power, manipulation, and control easily visible
within the prison institution, one can begin to see those same dynamics operating in the larger society. "One can use the prison system as a
magnifying glass through which one might see what is otherwise less
easily discernible in the culture—underlying patterns of motivation,
symbolization, and societal structure that determine the life of the community as a whole."[26]

Using the prison system as a magnifying glass enlarges one's
perspective on all parties involved, be they victim, perpetrator, or witness. The victim's condition and the crime inflicted, whether a violent
crime or a property crime, almost always reflects the ethics of shame
and honor embedded in society, described here only briefly, and all the
violence and violation that is generated by such an ethical imperative.
Then, if one takes the time to consider more carefully the circumstances
of the individual perpetrator, again, almost always, the power of shame
to generate and perpetuate violence and violation is not difficult to see
and understand. Further, if we are all always witnesses, we must possess
the clarity of vision and understanding as well as the courage to testify
to the truth of what we see and understand.

To see and understand the truth of the present retributive prison
system must be a call for action, a demand for change, a trumpet call for
transformation. If the present retributive prison system with its ethos of
punishment and shame only serves to expand, enlarge, and explode violence and crime, perhaps it is time for congregational prison ministries

25. Ibid., 189–90.
26. Ibid., 185.

to seriously consider the politics of Jesus. To be sure, Jesus admonished us to remember those who were in prison, but Jesus also called us to a radical transformation of the status quo. At the very least, with regard to prison ministry, we could begin to throw our weight on the side of genuine justice, a restorative model of justice whereby the health and wholeness of persons and community is primary. For it is only there and only then that we can begin to build that community that is called beloved here on this earth.

Building community through compassionate witnessing within congregational prison ministries may be the best hope for implementing transformation of the present retributive justice system, for together we can help one another grow in awareness, which, as Weingarten states, "builds the platform for future action."[27] We need not worry whether our action is big enough or important enough. What is essential is that together we find ways to begin to witness compassionately.

QUESTIONS FOR REFLECTION AND DISCUSSION

1. In reflecting on Kaethe Weingarten's premise that always we are all witnesses, do you think of yourself as a witness? Describe a situation when you were a witness. Were you empowered in the situation? How?

2. In the context of Weingarten's model, when have you experienced yourself as an empowered, aware witness? Empowered, unaware witness? Unempowered, aware witness? Unempowered, unaware witness?

3. Can you recall a time when you have occupied and/or acted from the role of victim, perpetrator, or witness? Reflect on the New Testament passage Luke 10: 30–35.

4. Consider the understanding of compassion p. 96. How do you imagine we might strengthen and support one another in the challenges of compassion? Are there instances of Jesus' ministry and his compassion that have been helpful to you?

5. What kinds of education and outreach can we provide our prison ministries in order to nurture our growth in aware and compassionate witnessing?

27. Weingarten, *Common Shock*, 34.

6

Three Models for Congregational Prison Ministry

Each time a person stands up for an idea, or acts to improve the lot
of others, or strikes out against injustice, [s]he sends forth a
tiny ripple of hope, and crossing each other from a million different
centers of energy and daring, those ripples build a current
that can sweep down the mightiest walls of oppression and resistance.

—ROBERT F. KENNEDY, "DAY OF AFFIRMATION ADDRESS,"
UNIVERSITY OF CAPETOWN, SOUTH AFRICA, JUNE 6, 1966

THE ORIGINAL PLAN

THE ORIGINAL PLAN FOR this final chapter was for the exploration of the concept of compassionate witnessing within two congregations as it related to prison ministry and the Partakers College Behind Bars program. The hope was that in demonstrating how to facilitate movement from witnessing positions of unaware to aware, from un-empowered to empowered, congregations would, indeed, become compassionate witnesses. A case study method was planned for a partnership between an urban black congregation and an urban white congregation in providing spiritual, financial, intellectual, and emotional support and commitment for a prisoner as he/she studied toward graduation in the Partakers College Behind Bars program. Not only would this facilitate awareness and empowerment among those inside and outside the walls of prison, at the same time, it would facilitate movement across boundaries of race and class. Over several months steps were taken to both explore and lay the foundation for this partnership. The urban, white congregation was a Quaker meeting; the urban, black congregation was a Baptist church. My initial expectation, perhaps a prejudging if you will, had been to assume that any resistance or unwillingness to participate in this partnership would come from the urban, black congregation. To my complete surprise, the opposite proved to be true. The black congregation embraced the idea of such a partnership.

Meanwhile, however, the proposal had come before the Ministry and Counsel Committee of the Quaker meeting to discuss and discern if the proposal should be brought before the larger meeting. It seemed that there was uneasiness with the proposal by one member of the committee, who interestingly was African American. As a young person, he had experienced white folks coming into the black inner city housing projects attempting to do good and instead they had caused more heartache and harm. It was his feeling that this white Quaker meeting was not ready to take on such a partnership as he did not believe they had honestly faced and worked through their own attitudes and experiences of racism. Since Quakers utilize the process of discernment, of seeking clearness and unity before coming to a decision, the objection of this one individual was felt to hinder that sense of clearness and unity, and so it was not possible to pursue the desired partnership.

However, as I continued along other paths for prison ministry, I engaged in new experiences, and it seemed that those experiences could well provide models for congregational prison ministry. It may be interesting to note that it is only in the past twenty years or so that the word *ministry* has been used in conjunction with prisons, creating the term *prison ministry*. As such, most often the purpose of such ministry is to bring the Good News of the gospel to prison inmates, to introduce them to the love of God, to evangelize them in the saving power of Jesus Christ. While all of this does indeed have its own value in the rehabilitation and lives of many prisoners, for many more prisoners much more is needed. It is one thing to attest to being "saved," to profess Jesus Christ as Lord and Savior while confined inside those walls, and quite another matter to carry that testimony outside the walls of prison when faced with no marketable skills, no affordable housing, and little community support. In the words of Martin Luther King Jr., "Any religion that professes to be concerned with the souls of men and is not concerned with the slums that damn them, the economic conditions that strangle them, and the social conditions that cripple them is a dry-as-dust religion."[1] The truth is that when it comes to prisons and prisoners, most religions are indeed as dry-as-dust.

To be sure, the issues are complex and seemingly overwhelming, but I know, unequivocally, that if we have the human knowledge and power to raise a 68,860 pound steel airplane into God's great blue skies, we most certainly have the human knowledge and power to solve any problem, however complex and overwhelming. As the late philosopher, E. F. Schumacher noted

> While the logical mind abhors divergent problems and tries to run away from them, the higher faculties of man accept the challenges of life as they are offered, without complaint, knowing that when things are most contradictory, absurd, difficult, and frustrating, then, *just then*, life really makes sense: as a mechanism provoking and almost forcing us to develop toward higher Levels of Being. The question is one of faith, of choosing our own "grade of significance." Our ordinary mind always tries to persuade us that we are nothing but acorns and that our greatest happiness will be to become bigger, fatter, shinier acorns, but that is of interest only to pigs. Our faith gives us knowledge of something much better: that we can become oak trees.[2]

Yes, it is our faith, not simply preached but rather lived in relationship to one another, lived in such a way that we do indeed help one another to become oak trees. It is hoped that the three models offered here may provide a broader understanding, a more encompassing view of how congregational prison ministries may come to care not only for the souls of men and women but for their minds, their hearts, their very lives as human brothers and sisters on this earth we share. While these models are not specifically reflective of restorative justice, they are reflective of ways to assist in humanizing the other, which does serve as an underlying principle of restorative justice practices.

1. King, *Words of Martin Luther King Jr.*, 66.
2. Schumacher, *Guide for the Perplexed*, 134–35.

MODEL ONE: PARTAKERS; CONGREGATIONAL PARTNERING WITH UNIVERSITY PRISON EDUCATION PROGRAMS

History of Partakers

It is said "a thousand mile journey begins with the first step," and the ten-year journey of Partakers, a faith-based prison ministry, began with a single woman, Jeannette Hanlon. By profession, Jeannette was a social worker, who lived in a comfortable suburb with her husband, an Episcopal minister, and their three children. She had never worked in a prison; indeed, she had never considered prison as a locale for her professional interests. However, unexpectedly one day, Jeannette was approached by a psychiatrist who worked at Bridgewater State Hospital for prisoners who asked her if she might consider working in the prisons. To be sure, this was a simple question but one which held an array of complex implications. Nevertheless, the question was posed at the right time and in the right place, and a seed was sown in fertile ground that would later give birth to the organization of Partakers.

Partakers was founded as a faith-based, not-for-profit organization, and it strives in several ways for reconciliation between prisoners and society. One primary and important avenue for such reconciliation has been to promote successful integration of prisoners into society by means of education, fostering connections between people inside and outside prison.

In January of 2000, Partakers initiated "College Behind Bars" as a pilot, in-prison higher education program. Working with Boston University's Prison Education Project, groups of volunteers were recruited to sponsor prisoners to pursue their college degrees while in prison. With the current prison population in the United States at record heights (there are now over two million inmates currently incarcerated at the state and federal level) a crisis of grave proportions confronts American society.

The Rise and Fall of Prison College Education Programs

Presently, there is very little in the way of rehabilitative programs for inmates. In 1990 there were 350 college prison programs. In 1997 there were seven, with Boston University's Prison Education Project being one of those remaining programs. Indeed, at the time even this program was struggling to continue serving prisoners in Massachusetts, for with the "get tough on crime" stance adopted by the United States Congress in 1995, all education Pell Grants for prisoners were eliminated. This meant that for nearly all of those 350 existing college programs inside prison facilities there was no financial reimbursement for the institutions and faculty who were providing such services, and as a result, they could no longer continue to assist prisoners towards achieving a college education.

There is a kind of strange irony in the way the sociopolitical pendulum swings. Twenty-five years ago, in September 1971, a revolt of prisoners erupted in the Attica prison in upstate New York. It is remembered as one of the bloodiest days in United States history, with twenty-nine prisoners and ten guards killed and scores of more prisoners shot, wounded, and beaten. The revolt was a cumulative reaction to years of growing abuse inside the prison walls, intolerable living and sleeping conditions, and lack of opportunity for education and rehabilitation. While the violence of the insurrection proved to be tragic, the publicity it generated proved to be beneficial in a variety of ways. One way was the availability of Pell Grants for college tuition loans for prisoners and the growth of college programs within prisons.

One such program originated within Boston University's Metropolitan College studies. In 1972, a professor emerita of English, Elizabeth Barker, began organizing poetry readings in local prisons. Her project developed into a comprehensive commitment to the power of reform through education, with approval from former Boston University President John Silber for the innovative Prison Education Program (PEP). Faculty members from Boston University now traveled to state prison facilities to teach liberal studies to inmates within prison classrooms. Soon other colleges, such as the University of Massachusetts, were extending similar services to inmates and within the next several years, additional programs sprung up throughout the country. Eagerly, inmates registered for classes. Professors found them hungry for learning; they were engaged and passionate students, respectful to one another and to their professors. Soon, with great pride and joy, hundreds of inmates throughout the country were receiving college diplomas.

By the mid-nineties, however, the sociopolitical pendulum was, once again, swinging in the opposite direction. There was now a new stance toward crime, a posture breeding fear and a punitive attitude toward prisoners. Indeed, such an attitude had already been generated several years earlier during the presidential candidacies of Richard Nixon and Barry Goldwater who were the first such individuals to politicize the issue of crime. By 1993 then, the climate was ripe for several members of the United States Congress to do likewise, as they played on the fears of the American public with their calls for a get-tough policy on crime, providing the impetus for the passage of the Violent Crime and Control Prevention Law, which now denied all prisoners access to Pell Grants.

The denial of higher education to prisoners highlights the common observation that human nature is a curious phenomenon. All too often it is our emotions that leap out ahead of our rational faculties. The denial of federal Pell Grants to prisoners is just one such example. The argument most often used supporting such denial is that there are thousands upon thousands of individuals within the lower socioeconomic class who have never committed a crime and yet cannot afford a college education, so why should a prisoner have access to a college education? Why should federal funds for higher education be diverted to prisoners, depleting the reserve of money available for those on the outside? While the premises of the argument *appear* logical, they are, in fact quite illogical. The truth is that in this land of touted equality, the opportunity for higher education should be available to *all*; one group within the lower socioeconomic class need not be pitted against another within that same class. Yet, this is exactly what happens as psychiatrist James Gilligan notes in his book, *Violence: Reflections on a National Epidemic.* In his excellent analysis of poverty and crime and its reflections on the political/socioeconomic class system in the United States, Gilligan provides a clear understanding of the vested interest the higher ruling class has in generating fear of the poor criminal among the middle and lower classes. States Gilligan,

> For the more that people are worried about crime and violence, the more the middle class will focus its anger and fear on the poor and members of certain minority groups (for most of the violence that is labeled as "crime" is committed by people from those groups); the nonviolent and noncriminal poor will be angry at those other people who are violent criminals; and both those classes will be too distracted by their anger at the lower-class criminals to notice that they have much better reasons to be angry at the very rich, and the party that represents the interests of the rich, than at all the violent criminals put together.[3]

3. Gilligan, *Violence*, 186–87.

With regard to the denial of federal Pell Grants for prisoners, the fomenting of anger and fear among the middle and lower classes was exactly what happened. The fact that less than one-tenth of 1 percent of Pell Grant funding was allotted to prisoners was a fact that was little known. Other facts not generally known are that higher education is *the* most effective method of crime prevention and recidivism. Gilligan states, "Nothing decreases the rate of crime and violence as powerfully and effectively as does education. We know that the single most effective factor which reduces the rate of recidivism in the prison population is education, and yet education in the prisons is the first item to be cut when an administration 'gets tough on crime.'"[4]

Lack of education and imprisonment go hand in hand. The average prisoner is functionally illiterate, has never had a steady job, has a background of juvenile delinquency and substance abuse, and in all likelihood has come from a dysfunctional home setting, where he or she suffered physical and/or sexual abuse. If, however, a prisoner has the opportunity to pursue a college education while incarcerated, the chances of attaining and keeping employment after release increase exponentially, and the recidivism rate decreases to nearly zero. Indeed, the evidence is clear and powerful. With 97 percent of prisoners returning to society and with 40 to 46 percent of those released returning to prison, it is in the best interests of all to support in-prison higher education. The fact is that using taxpayer money to educate prisoners is the best possible assurance towards the reduction of criminal activity and the creation of safe communities. It is not a question of whether or not prisoners deserve a college education. Rather, providing the opportunity for prisoners to obtain higher education just makes good sense, for it is clear that in the long run everyone benefits.

My Experience with Partakers

My own experience with Partaker's has certainly underscored the benefits that a higher education provides for prisoners and the transformative possibilities inherent in that education. In the fall of 2003, I began an internship with Partakers as part of my doctoral studies in ministry at Andover Newton Theological School. The founder of Partakers and my intern supervisor, Jeannette Hanlon, provided me with a mandate to

4. Ibid., 188.

form a support group of both faculty and students at Andover Newton Theological School for a prisoner in the Partakers College Behind Bars program in conjunction with the Boston University Prison Education Project. I was asked to make an initial visit to a young woman at Framingham State Prison who had applied to the program, an individual who Jeannette was not at all sure would be suitable as she had been in and out of "the hole," a term referring to the place of solitary confinement. Indeed, Jeannette wondered if this woman might have serious psychiatric illness that would prevent her from active and successful participation in the program. My task was to meet with her and make an assessment followed by a recommendation.

Initial Visit to Framingham State Prison

The first day I traveled to the prison was a beautiful blue-sky September day. As I drove into the parking lot, I could feel the rising apprehension inside of me. I looked at my watch and then began the mental checklist in preparation for entering the prison: watch off, ring off, earrings off, drivers license out of my wallet, car registration out of the glove compartment, quarters out of my change purse, a five dollar bill out of my billfold, car keys and writing pen in hand, pocketbook locked in the trunk. Hoping I had it all down correctly, I headed across the parking lot to the front entrance. I could feel the heaviness weighing in my heart. Entering those doors is not easy because of all that is contained within those walls.

Inside the lobby waiting area, I took a seat. On this first visit, Laura Tuach, the assistant director of Partakers, had agreed to meet me there and to guide me through the process of gaining entry to the prison. I had never met her, but she had told me she had shoulder-length blond hair, so I waited and watched as folks gathered in the waiting area. Soon, a young, attractive, blonde-haired woman walked in, and with eye contact, we recognized one another. Laura explained that we needed to wait for someone to arrive at the desk to hand out the information forms we would need to complete. As we waited, Laura explained that she is never her usual outgoing self while going through this process. Instead, she is watchful, cautious, with a certain level of anxiety. How long will the wait be? Will there be any unexpected obstacles? Will there be any difficult encounters? Will it not be possible to get in? I am relieved to know that some of the uneasiness and apprehension I am feeling is understandable.

By now there are a dozen or so of us in the lobby waiting area. It's been more than a half hour since I arrived. At last there is someone behind the glass partition handing out the visitor forms. Laura helps me to complete the form and explains the process they use for numbering the forms and calling visitors into the "trap," the screening area each visitor must pass through before entering the visiting room. Soon Laura is called in; she is visiting another prisoner who is enrolled in the Partakers College Behind Bars program. Finally, after another fifteen minutes, I too am called forward. Inside, I am given a plastic box and told to take my shoes off and walk through the metal detector. It all feels strange; I too am watchful, cautious, and somewhat anxious. The guard who is in charge of this piece of the process is stone-faced and abrupt. She stamps my hand and opens the inner door for me to enter the inmate waiting area. But I am still in my stocking feet. "What about my shoes?" I ask. "Oh," she exclaims, "I forgot to give them back to you. I don't do this often anymore. I'm just filling in today." Somehow there is a relaxation of the barriers that seem to separate us. The rules and regulations seem to have softened, and in that moment her forgetfulness has allowed her humanity to feel more real.

Upon entering, I quickly scan the room trying to determine who this inmate, Lynne, may be. I find a seat along the back wall facing out to the visiting area so I can observe the entire space. I see Laura sitting further down along the side wall to my right; she appears deeply engaged with the young woman she is visiting. Closer to my right are two others, a mother, it seems, and her daughter. Then I see another Partakers volunteer who had joined us earlier in the outer waiting area and watch as she connects with the inmate she has come to visit.

Meanwhile I sit, waiting for Lynne to arrive. One of the guards has moved from the desk to a table and chair further over to my left as if to keep a closer watch on everyone. There is no interaction with any of us in the room. Their faces are expressionless except during the occasional conversation they engage in with one another. I think of the passage from Walter Wink's book *Engaging the Powers*:

> The Powers are good.
> The Powers are fallen.
> The Powers must be redeemed.[5]

---

5. Wink, *Engaging the Powers*, 10.

I have already been waiting a half hour. I try to sit quietly as if in Quaker meeting for worship, keeping the stillness and quiet within me. A young couple who were in the outer waiting room on my arrival are also still waiting. Just then, an older woman, perhaps in her forties or fifties comes into the room and shuffles over to them and begins to weep. I cannot hear their conversation. Could it be their mother I wonder? My own heart weeps for all the sorrow and suffering of the lives of these individuals. I consider the words of James Gilligan, "Punishing requires much less effort than does understanding the many different forms of violence."[6] His words ring true. To understand these people here, these families, these individuals, the complexity of their lives, the forces that have shaped them would require enormous resources of time and effort. It would require a stretching of human consciousness and human compassion, which to date, we are unable and or unwilling to engage in.

It is now nearly an hour since I have been waiting. I consider going up to the guards at the desk, but I remember Laura saying one just goes in and sits down and waits for the inmate to arrive. By now I am feeling a bit uneasy and hope that Lynne does not come much later because then it would overlap into the change of shifts, and as Laura noted, no one can enter or leave during that time. Perhaps the visitor and inmate to my right, a mother and daughter it would seem, have sensed my uneasiness. The inmate asks whom I am waiting for and suggests I go up and ask the guard, warning me, "If you don't ask, they'll let you sit here forever."

Going up to the desk, I inquire and am informed that they had already called upstairs once but agree to call again. I continue to wait until at last they call me back to the desk and explain that Lynne is on restriction until the seventh of October, stating that I should have been informed of this when I registered in the outer lobby. The guard asks if I am ready to leave and offers to call another guard to let me out. I wait at the door with the guard as he calls on the phone to the outside desk. They don't answer right away. I wait a little longer side by side with this correctional officer, and I can feel my own protective inner guard in place. He comments about the new system for exiting the waiting area, "It used to be easier," he says. He is young, maybe in his thirties, with light brown hair and blue eyes—nice looking, I think. Now I can feel my inner guard easing, and I see him in his humanity.

---

6. Gilligan, *Violence*, 24.

Outside in the lobby I head for the large window. I want to leave, to get outside, but Laura is still inside and I worry she may come out and wonder where I am. For another fifteen minutes I stand by the window looking out at trees and blue sky, trying to keep all that I'm feeling under control, trying to sort it all out in my mind. At last, Laura comes out. We retrieve our belongings from the locker space and head outside, out into the open air. I drink it in, keenly aware of my own freedom.

A Relationship with Lynne Begins

A few days later, I heard from Jeannette Hanlon. She had received a letter from Lynne stating she would not be available for a visit as she was in "the hole." Jeannette was apologetic that the letter had not arrived in time to prevent me from an unnecessary trip to the prison. While I might have spent the time in another more productive way, it had not been wasted time. The experience of that first visit proved useful as it prepared me for my next visit to Lynne a few weeks later. I knew from her introductory letter to Partakers that she was "36 years of age, had long brown hair, stood at 5´4˝ and weighed 135 pounds with pretty blue-green eyes." She, too, had received my own letter of introduction, and so when she walked into the prison waiting room, we quickly recognized one another.

She had begun her first correspondence course, and we talked about the course contents and requirements, the timetable she had set for herself for completion of this course, and her plans for the second one. Her hope was that she would be able to complete the three required correspondence courses by the end of December and apply for admission for the next semester of the Boston University program that would begin in January. She was not at all sure of her ability to reach this goal, and though I had only just met her, I sensed an inner strength and determination about her, and as I listened I tried to be encouraging and supportive. Sharing with her my own student experience, I hoped would be helpful. It became clear to me that Lynne was articulate and obviously quite smart. She had an energetic and feisty spirit; I liked her.

While part of my purpose was to form a support group of other divinity students and faculty, simultaneously I began to visit Lynne every three weeks. As she continued in her studies, I learned more about her life before she was imprisoned as well as her day-to-day life inside the prison; neither were pleasant experiences. Lynne had been sentenced to life with the option of parole after fifteen years. By the time I began to visit her, she had served five years of that sentence. At times, I found it difficult to listen to the realities of her life in prison. It was all so oppressive and at times seemed to get in the way of her focusing on her studies. I wanted to be a supportive listener but at the same time it seemed important not to get too immersed in the negative, psychologically sick dynamics of the prison culture. The opportunity to reflect on my experience with Jeannette and the other student interns in my Partaker's group who were also visiting prisoners was enormously helpful in maintaining a good perspective and balance as I continued my visits to Lynne.

By the beginning of December, Lynne was into the last of her three correspondence courses but having a difficult time. She was faithful with the required reading, would complete the required paper, and send it off to the professor only to have it returned with disparaging comments and criticisms. She was feeling angry and discouraged, not at all sure she would be able to make the end of December deadline for completing the applications for admission into the Boston University program. I listened patiently, acknowledging the legitimacy of her feelings, and then admonished her, "Do not let these feelings get in the way of your goals. Just make the corrections and send it back and just keep moving forward. I'm rooting for you!" Then, just before my scheduled visit in late January, I had a letter from Lynne. She had received news of her admission to Boston University; she had registered for her first two courses and would begin classes in a few weeks. I was elated, so happy for her and so very proud of her! For over four years now I have visited Lynne once a month. From time to time her support group has had a few professors and a few other students, most of whom have moved on in the course of their own studies. Presently, one other professor and I visit faithfully, writing to Lynne between our visits. Lynne has become an important part of our lives, and as she gives testimony in the following excerpts from a letter she wrote recently to Partakers, we too have become an important part of her life.

> Hi, my name is Lynne and I am currently serving a life sentence. I started the Partakers program three years ago. The program helped me to earn the credits needed for me to start the Boston University Prison Education Project. I wasn't sure how I felt at first about meeting and having visits from people I really didn't know. However, I have turned it into the best experience of my life. The two women who come to visit me are amazing. One

woman, Joanne has become a major part of my life. I can't imagine life without her. The encouragement and support she has given me has gotten me to where I am today. I have earned 77 credits and all my grades are As and Bs. Any information I need to help me with my classes, she is there to supply happily. Sharon, my other sponsor, has recently been able to become more involved in my life which has been great. Her spirit and enthusiasm has managed to make me smile at some of the most difficult times. The Partakers program has helped numerous women attain an education that not only will help them when they leave, but has helped them in prison. Before I started the program I spent a lot of time getting into trouble. The program has given me the chance to see myself as a better person, a person who can become someone of importance in life. My mind is learning and I enjoy it. I would never have believed I was smart but with the faith from my sponsors and the program I have found that I am. I can become a better person. I can do something constructive with my life that I can be proud of. I thank everyone who has made this opportunity possible for me. Words can't begin to express my gratitude.[7]

Certainly Lynne's words testify to the documented research that prison college programs are among the best possible means to reduce recidivism. Presently there are over two million persons in prison in the United States, and the cost of housing each of those individuals is over thirty-two million dollars per year. The Partakers College Behind Bars program in conjunction with the Boston University Prison Education project is three thousand dollars. The math is quite simple. In dollar terms, prison college education just makes good sense. It is really quite simple for faith communities to become involved in this mentoring program. First, a church agrees to pay the cost of the three correspondence courses, which a prisoner must enroll in prior to applying to the Boston University program and then form a support group of four to six church members who agree to visit the prisoner (usually in teams of two) once a month, as well as to correspond by mail with the prisoner, to offer educational, emotional, and spiritual support as he or she embarks on this road to higher education. In human terms, both for individual human beings and for the human community at large, the measure of worth is, as Lynne states, "beyond words to describe."

7. Lynne, letter to Partakers, November, 2006.

MODEL TWO: THE ALTERNATIVES
TO VIOLENCE PROJECT

History of the Alternatives to Violence Project

In 1975, within the New York prison system, the Alternatives to Violence Project, or AVP, was initiated at the request of a group of inmates in Greenhaven Prison. This particular group of inmates was known as the Think Tank, and they had been designated to be counselors in an experimental program for underage offenders. They recognized their need for nonviolence training to prepare them for this work and knowing of Quaker's peace and nonviolence testimonies, asked a local Quaker group to assist them. From this beginning the AVP program spread to other prisons within the United States, then to the outside community, and eventually to prison and nonprison groups internationally. The AVP program can now be found in most states and in more than twenty countries.

At its inception, the focus of AVP was on prisons, on finding ways to reduce the violence within prisons, assisting people to survive such violence, and equally important, helping individuals reduce the violence in their own lives. Early on it became clear that the violence found in the prison system is quite simply a reflection of the violence that is lodged in our larger society, our institutions, and our values. As James Gilligan states, "The prisons are not only a laboratory for the study of violence, but a subterranean index of much of what is both expressed in our wider culture, and at the same time, buried deep within the collective unconscious of patriarchal culture."[8] Whether we wish to acknowledge it or not, all of us are capable of violence, and this is a basic underlying premise of AVP. Acknowledging this reality allows us to begin to name the places of violence in our own lives, both the individual violence and the cultural violence.

AVP is an experiential program; it engages all the participants to seek and share, recognizing that it is not possible to provide answers for another person. Rather, by creating a safe, encouraging, affirming environment, individuals are able to seek within themselves the solutions they need to live a more self-fulfilling life, growing into their God-given gifts and human potential. Empowering individuals in this way within the context of AVP emanates from the belief that

8. Gilligan, *Violence*, 180.

there is in the universe a power that is able to transform hostility and destructiveness into cooperation and community, and to do justice among us. We believe that the power is everywhere—in us, in our opponents, and in the world around us. We believe that it is possible to tune into it, and that if we do, it will enable us and our opponents to realize our birthright of peace and dignity. We believe that there are certain individual and group dynamics that make it possible to tune into this power; and that these dynamics can be learned and used by all people everywhere to build more constructive lives and healthier societies.[9]

With this foundational belief, the mission of AVP is to seek to reduce interpersonal violence by providing conflict management skills, in which people learn the value of affirmation, respect, community building, cooperation, and trust. By fostering personal insights; promoting growth and awareness that improves relationships with self, other, and the world; and offering experiential workshops, AVP empowers people to lead nonviolent lives.[10]

Design of the Alternatives to Violence Project

The design of AVP generally consists of several activities extended over a total time frame of twenty hours. AVP is first and foremost an experiential program, composed of various exercises that facilitate the learning of nonviolent behavior with the use of role playing. The facilitators of the program are volunteers, many of whom are seasoned and dedicated individuals who are deeply committed to the underlying philosophy of AVP. Equally significant to the success of the program is the voluntary participation of the individuals who take part in the program. This is particularly important in the setting of the prison where inmates may feel under pressure by the administration to take part in the workshops as a requirement for parole or obtaining credits for "good time." At the outset of each workshop the importance of voluntary participation is made clear because individuals can only learn, change, and grow if they choose to do so.

The model for AVP workshops is one of team leadership. There are two lead facilitators and two or three other facilitators; all share in the planning and implementation of the workshop. Within the prison

9. AVP/USA, *AVP Manual Basic Course*, A-2.
10. Ibid., A-4.

setting, the leadership team is comprised of both inmates and outside facilitators. On completion of the basic weekend training, one can proceed to the advanced weekend training workshop, and then take part in the training for facilitators weekend. It is during this last workshop that participants get hands-on practice in their experience of facilitating AVP. Then, after completion of all three workshops, individuals receive their certificate endorsing them as AVP facilitators.

Empowering people and training them to be leaders is an essential element of AVP. It is a model that eschews hierarchy. Instead, it fosters community, cooperation, and trust; all decisions are made by consensus. While the techniques and exercises are extremely useful in providing the necessary training to cope with violence, AVP acknowledges that the true source of nonviolence is spiritual power. This power, basic to all religious beliefs, lies within each human being, and this power forms the central foundation of AVP. It is designated *Transforming Power*.

Transforming Power is difficult to define. It is best described by those who have experienced it, and those experiences are varied and unique to each individual and each situation. Certainly, it is known as a power that is able to change the shape and outcome of a violent and destructive encounter into a cooperative and constructive outcome. It is able to work through human beings if there is an openness to its presence and power. It means a willingness to lay aside previous assumptions about the necessity of violence to produce a winning outcome and to lay aside previous assumptions about the character of the other individual. It means a willingness to listen inwardly to oneself as well as outwardly to truly hear what the other person is saying. It means a willingness to offer a caring and compassionate response and to seek common ground. One must believe that a positive outcome is possible whereby all parties involved feel successful in the resolution of the conflict.

The title *Alternatives to Violence* may well be the best descriptive term for the program, implying as it does behavioral options to conflict resolution. All too often, unfortunately, the term *nonviolence* holds the negative connotation of passivity or submissiveness. This, however, is a misconception. Theologian Walter Wink is very clear when he states that, "Nonviolence is not idealistic or sentimental about evil; it does not coddle or cajole aggressors but moves against perceived injustice proactively."[11] Nonviolence has as a basic tenet respect for self and re-

11. Wink, *Powers That Be*, 121.

spect for the other person, an acknowledgement and assertion of one's own rights as well as the rights of the other person and seeks justice for all parties involved in the resolution of a conflict. The Alternatives to Violence program assists all of us in the human family to grow in our ability to discover and utilize the means of resolving conflict with care, cooperation, and creativity.

Experiencing an AVP Weekend in the Prison Setting

As a Quaker, I had heard about AVP for years and had always known that it was something in which I would like to participate. Always, however, there seemed to be other priorities vying for my time and attention. With the beginning of my doctoral studies, however, and my internship with Partakers (who along with sponsoring the College Behind Bars program, also sponsored volunteers in AVP within the prison setting) it seemed timely for my participation in AVP training.

It was a weekend in late September, and the prison where the workshop would take place was in a medium-security facility west of Boston. Set as it was at the end of a narrow country road in a wooded area that then opened into a valley with gentle rolling slopes and tall evergreens reaching up towards open blue sky, the freedom of the natural setting seemed in stark contrast to the barbed wire fencing, steel gates, and harshness of the red-brick prison buildings. Why, I wondered, did I always feel such heaviness in my spirit when encountering the prison complex?

The weekend workshop began at five o'clock on Friday evening and the introductory session closed at nine. On Saturday and Sunday the sessions were scheduled from eight until four, and on those days we would share lunch with the inmates. On this particular weekend there were two outside facilitators and two inmate facilitators. Four of us would enter as outside participants in the workshop, and the remaining participants, about sixteen men, inmates of the prison, would comprise the group for this basic AVP training workshop. I don't believe any of us had any clear, detailed sense of what the weekend would entail, only that one had to choose an adjective name. In the lobby waiting area of the prison we met the two outside facilitators who would lead us; their adjective names were Natural Nancy and Amazing Anita. Certainly, the four of us participating for the first time from the outside, all working and or studying in the ministry, had concluded that simply by virtue of the title of the program, *Alternatives to Violence*, there had to be value to the weekend training.

Those of us who were entering from the outside had cleared through the "trap" and had been escorted through the prison yard to one of the brick buildings and into a small classroom. We had begun to gather the hard plastic chair–type desks into a circle when the group of inmates filed in. At once it began to feel crowded, but we were told that we would only gather in this room for this first evening session and that for the remaining two days we would be in a large open room more conducive for the format of the workshop.

A Beginning Framework for Our AVP Weekend

As we all took our seats, one could sense the uneasy awkwardness among this group of strangers in this anomalous setting. Together, the outside facilitators and the inmate facilitators introduced themselves with a short opening talk, a review of the agenda for the weekend and the setting forth of the ground rules. These were important and essential ingredients for the framework of the weekend, and everyone needed to agree to abide by them. No one could criticize him- or herself or anyone else; no one could interrupt a person who was speaking; no one could volunteer another person; each person had the right to forego participation in any particular session; and, vitally important, strict confidentiality was to be observed.

Thus far, a more formal and serious atmosphere prevailed, but what followed next initiated a change that was invitation to fun and informality. The contrast between these two modes of being would prevail throughout the weekend. Gathered around the circle, each person had to introduce him- or herself using a positive adjective name, a word that started with the same letter of the alphabet as their own name. That seemed easy enough, but then we were told that before you introduced yourself, you needed to repeat back the adjective names of all those in the circle who had already introduced themselves! A clamor of groans and cries went up in the face of what seemed an impossible task, but Natural Nancy offered to begin, and as she had the very simple task of only stating her own name, she agreed to repeat back all twenty-three other names when we had completed the circle. It was great fun to hear which adjective name a person would choose and what a wonderful variety we had! There was Cool Calvin, Distinguished Damien, Nice Nate, and I was Jubilant Joanne! By the time we were finished there had been a good deal of laughter and good-natured joshing. We were building a sense of community.

Next came "a gathering." These times would be interspersed throughout the weekend, a time to come together in the circle for more serious reflection and sharing. Now, we were asked to go around the circle and state one thing we each hoped to get from the weekend, and then after a short break we returned to another exercise introduced as "Light and Livelies." As the name implies, we entered into a time of fun and frolic. We came to realize that these activities, which provided energy and humor, helped balance our more sedentary, serious, and sometimes heavy times of sharing and reflection. We all grew to eagerly anticipate our Light and Livelies! This evening we engaged in the L&L titled, "I Love You Baby, but I Just Can't Smile." One inmate began by sitting in a chair looking very glum. One by one we tried to make him laugh. Forbidden to laugh, he responded to our efforts saying, "I love you baby, but I just can't smile." He, of course, was trying to make one of us laugh. However, if he himself laughed he was out of the game, and whoever made him laugh now took his place. Some were very stoic and able to hold their nonlaughing position for several minutes. Eventually it seemed impossible not to laugh, at which point we would all be laughing and having great fun!

Next, we gathered in two circles with two people facing each other for an affirmation-in-pairs exercise. Each person in the pair spoke to his or her partner for three minutes on the topic, "What I like about myself." The partner was to listen carefully, not responding, only reminding the person, if necessary, to refrain from any negative comments. At the end of the three minutes, the pair reversed roles. Finally, everyone came together again in the larger circle when each of the pairs introduced their partner to the whole group. Clearly, by the end of this exercise new energy was palpable among all of us in the room.

Now, we moved to a more serious reflection as our facilitators stood at the head of the circle and invited everyone to brainstorm in drawing first, a tree of violence, which would include definitions of violence, human emotions, and circumstances that contribute to violence. Then, we all contributed to drawing a tree of nonviolence, imagining what such a tree as that would include. For nearly an hour we engaged in this reflection with a growing appreciation of the many ways we are conditioned to violence in both our personal lives and within the larger society. After taking a brief time to evaluate our first evening session, we closed with an affirmation pyramid, standing to join in a tight circle, with one person after another stretching one hand upward into the middle of the circle, one hand on top of another as each person affirmed one thing they received from the evening, culminating in a celebratory "Whoop!" As we all parted with good-byes and goodnights, the warmth, energy, and camaraderie shared spoke eloquently to the newly felt sense of community among all of us, insiders and outsiders.

Our Second Day of AVP Shared with Inmates

On Saturday morning, having laid a good foundation for community the evening before, we came together no longer strangers, but as companions on this weekend journey. For these next two days our workshops would take place in a larger community room, giving us a lot more space for the various exercises we would engage in. While at first it seemed the day loomed long ahead of us, the morning went by all too quickly as we engaged in exercises of Concentric Circles, Empathy Exercises, Quick Decisions and, of course, Light and Livelies, which we all looked forward to!

For those of us from the outside, sharing lunch with this group of inmates was an experience in and of itself. Sitting at small tables with four or five of these men was an opportunity to talk informally, to ask questions about their life inside prison, to listen as they shared aspects of their own journeys, and to further dismantle prejudices and stereotypes. It also provided considerable appreciation of the poor quality of food these men were served at mealtimes day in and day out. Though they were quick to make jokes about it, simultaneously apologizing to us, it was easy to see that this aspect of prison life only served to deepen the infliction of their punishment.

After lunch we came back into our circle for a gathering. This time was spent in sharing around the topic, "a way I deal with my anger," and this was a perfect focus to move into the essence of AVP, a session on Transforming Power. The facilitators began by explaining the concept as the power we all have to move a situation in a positive direction toward resolution of conflict, and sharing examples of such times in their own lives. Then we moved into small groups to reflect and share with one another a conflict we were able to resolve nonviolently. Using the copy of the *Guide to Transforming Power* with the twelve criteria listed (e.g., reach for that something good in others; be ready to revise your position if it is wrong; use surprise and humor; build community based on honesty, respect, and caring), assisted us as we shared and listened to one another's experiences. When we returned to the larger circle to report, discuss, and process each group's encounters, our discoveries and insights into self and other were deepened still further. Most certainly, by this time we were all ready for a break and another Light and Lively!

Reenergized now, it was well into the afternoon, and we separated again into small groups. Each group was given a box of Tinkertoys with instructions to choose a model shown on the box to build together. For the first five minutes, without opening the Tinkertoy box, we were free to talk among ourselves about our plan and how we would proceed. Then in silence, signaling to each other nonverbally, we worked together for the next twenty minutes to create our model. When time was called, each group shared the process they had experienced: their feelings, the participation of the members, emerging leadership, frustrations, and emerging patterns of cooperation.

Finally, another break, another Light and Lively, an end-of-the-day evaluation, and our closing circle, going around with each person free to offer an affirmation of another member of the group, completing the sentence of, "I see in you the gift of . . . " Was I tired? Yes, but all of us were clearly energized and empowered and looking forward to returning the next morning.

Our Last Day of AVP: A Profound Experience

Early on Sunday morning as we gathered together in our circle, we reviewed the agenda for the day. A few of the facilitators were busy hanging large, blank sheets of poster paper all around one end of the room. We learned that these were "Affirmation Posters." Each of us, using colorful markers, would write our adjective name on the top of one of the sheets, and then throughout the day during our short breaks or our longer lunch break we would write an affirming note on each person's poster. As the day progressed, each sheet became a rainbow of messages.

The opening of our early morning circle, however, was an experience most profound and deeply spiritual. Everyone had been invited to bring something to share, a picture, a poem, a song. Several of the inmates brought pictures of family, passing them around the circle, sharing a family story. A few read poems written from their own sorrow and struggle of living life outside as well as inside the confines of prison. The depth of sharing and the power permeating that circle transcended all barriers between "us and them," of offender and nonoffender.

With new exercises, a few breaks, lunch, and Light and Livelies, the hours flew by. The key event of the afternoon were role plays, the purpose of which was to enact a situation that could lead to nonviolent and fair resolution of a conflict using the Transforming Power guidelines. Having been divided into four groups, each group went off to create their role play, and after sufficient time for discussion and planning, the presentations got underway. The ingenuity and creativity of each group was unique; the "audience" was intrigued as each role play unfolded, and almost always there was much humor interspersed amidst a situation that was most serious. With the end of each role play, there was time for debriefing and discussion, with new understandings and insights shared.

Then, taking time for a well-deserved break we joined once again in our circle for a final gathering, sharing round the circle "an insight I have received from this workshop." One could feel a small bit of sadness as we realized our time together was nearing an end, at which time our facilitators invited us to a last Light and Lively . . . just what the moment called for! "Big Wind Blows" proved to be great fun. Having made the circle short of one chair, one of our facilitators, designated as Big Wind, stood in the middle of our circle. Taking a moment for consideration, he then called out, "Big Wind blows on everyone who is wearing white sneakers." All those in the circle wearing white sneakers had to move to a new chair; Big Wind had to find a chair also! Whoever was left standing without a chair was now Big Wind, who now called out, "Big Wind blows on everyone who has brown eyes." Once again there was a mad movement, a search for a new seat; lots of energy, lots of fun!

Finally, settling down in a full circle once again, we took time for a shared evaluation of the whole weekend workshop. All seemed to reflect a sense of satisfaction, time well spent, great insights, valuable experience. Standing at the head of the circle, the facilitators took turns calling each participant forward to receive their certificate for completion of this basic training in AVP. Watching these men go forward with enthusiasm and pride, amidst loud cheers and applause, to receive their certificate moved me to joy and tears. Even more remarkable was the experience of retrieving my affirmation poster and reading all the positive endorsements of value and appreciation signed by these fellows such as:

> "I thank you sincerely for coming here and sharing with us to help us all grow. I appreciate it very much."

> "Thank you for being here. We're going to miss you big."

> "It is people like you that helped me change from who I was to who I am and who I will be. Thank you."

> "Thank you very much. You have been inspirational to me. May God bless you for many, many, many more years to come."

Lots of hugs, good-bye and good-luck wishes, our parting was such sweet sorrow as these men headed in one direction back through the security gate into their living compound, and we headed in another direction through a different security gate towards the exiting building, still waving to one another across the barbed wire fencing that separated us. My heart grew heavy again. Yes, it was important and necessary that individuals who commit harm be held accountable for their actions, be able to learn from their mistakes, and yes, there are individuals who, for reasons so deep seated in their psyche and experience, may need to be separated out from the larger society indefinitely. Still, I felt certain with a deep inner knowing that something was wrong with this system of punishment. Perhaps my knowing is reflected in the words of former prison psychiatrist, James Gilligan when he states, "punishment beyond what is necessary for *restraint* (the punishment of retribution, or vengeance) is an ill-conceived, misdirected, societal crime for which we pay dearly in lives, suffering, and societal costs."[12]

Completion of my AVP Training

Over the next several months, I returned to the prison to complete my advanced training weekend and my training for facilitators weekend and finally a weekend where I was one of the facilitators and at last received my final certificate endorsing me as a full-fledged AVP facilitator!

The in-prison AVP experience takes one beyond appearances, beyond exterior boundaries, beyond limiting stereotypes into deep, rewarding, rich personal growth and empowerment whether one lives on

12. Gilligan, *Violence*, 140.

the inside or outside of prison. Indeed, similar to one of the guidelines of Transforming Power, "reach for that something good in others," is the insight from *The Little Prince* by Antoine de Saint-Exupery, "One sees clearly only with the heart. Anything essential is invisible to the eyes."[13] Such growth and empowerment, however small or large, ultimately works together to provide healing and transformation within persons, communities, and the world. Surely, this is what Jesus was about in his life and teaching. Surely, this is what church congregations need be about. Indeed, with the recognition that the United States is the most violent nation in the industrialized world, with the highest murder rate, with the recognition that by the age of twelve the average child has witnessed twelve thousand murders via the multiple avenues of the media, it would seem to be imperative for church congregations to actively engage in promoting alternatives to violence. The education and experience provided through AVP offers a most valuable framework and foundation towards achieving this new paradigm of engaging with ourselves and our world.

MODEL THREE: COMMITTEE OF FRIENDS
AND RELATIVES OF PRISONERS

History of the Committee of Friends and Relatives of Prisoners

The Committee of Friends and Relatives of Prisoners (CFROP) located in Boston, Massachusetts takes its roots from the first CFROP formed in 1977 on Long Island in Suffolk County, New York. At that time, at the Suffolk County, New York's local jail, historic legal battles had ensued over issues of unconstitutional treatment of inmates. A Long Island group dedicated to equal justice issues was now advocating for prisoners' rights and had filed a lawsuit in the United States District Court for the Eastern District of New York. Additionally, they had organized an informational picket line at the jail to publicize the jail's noncompliance with court orders, and with this they began to receive calls and requests for help from both prisoners in the local jail and from their families and friends on the outside.

With the growing unrest inside the jail, with prisoner grievances regarding the lack of medical treatment and the spread of tuberculosis inside

13. Saint-Exupery, *Little Prince*, 63.

the jail, family members and friends of these inmates called a meeting. As a result of their organizing, three hundred people came together, and a decision was made to form a separate organization of friends and relatives as well as concerned individuals to address the problems that lead to incarceration as well as the problems that result from incarceration. This organization would be known as the Committee of Friends and Relatives of Prisoners (CFROP) and included individual organizers who had been trained in all-volunteer, community-based, grass-roots efforts. As a free and voluntary private membership organization, the CFROP mission is to promote self-help efforts to benefit families and friends of prisoners and their loved ones behind bars, understanding full well that the problems on the inside have their roots in the problems on the outside. Indeed, they are inseparable, clearly connected, and cyclical.

Founder of CFROP/Boston: Harold Adams

Perhaps, no one could understand this interconnection better than Harold Adams, the Operations Manager of the CFROP located in Boston, Massachusetts. Harold Adams is a former prisoner, sentenced to life, incarcerated for thirty years, who was then paroled in 2002. Harold grew up in the impoverished neighborhoods of Harlem and as a teenager began running the streets, becoming involved with drugs and crime. With his incarceration as a young adult, slowly his perspective on life, on people, and on society began to change. Very quickly he sensed that if he was to survive within those prison walls, he was going to need a survival strategy. Rather simultaneously, and perhaps serendipitously, a math textbook was placed in his hands, and he decided that page by page, chapter by chapter, he would teach himself the concepts of math contained in those pages. For Harold, this was the beginning of both his intellectual development and his personal transformation. In the years that followed, he completed his GED, enrolled in college classes, and through the Boston University Prison Education Project, graduated summa cum laude. He received the honor of being invited to be class valedictorian but, as might be expected, was prohibited by the Department of Corrections to leave the prison in order to take part in the graduation ceremonies. He was, however, chosen to be runner-up class valedictorian and later, after his release, was invited to travel to Tuscany, Italy, as an apprentice mathematician, to take part in a two-week seminar sponsored by the Advanced Studies Institute of NATO.

Those long months and years spent in reading and reflecting, in studying and self-education gave Harold a clear and deep experiential understanding that there are two systems of justice in this country—one for the poor and one for the rich. As author Jeffrey Reiman states, "The *weeding out of the wealthy* starts at the very entrance to the criminal justice system: The decision about whom to investigate, arrest, or charge is not made on the basis of the offense committed or the danger posed. It is a decision distorted by a systematic economic bias that works to the disadvantage of the poor."[14] This truth is supported by the United States Bureau of Prisons own estimate that 85 percent of individuals in United States prisons are poor. One may then conclude that, in a very real sense, it is a crime to be poor.

The Work of CFROP

Such truths and the conclusions that follow from those truths provide the foundation for the work of CFROP. While the Committee of Friends and Relatives of Prisoners is an organization on the outside, there is the clear acknowledgement that the struggle inside and the struggle outside start from the same place. When a breadwinner of a family, be it a father or a mother, is incarcerated, the economic impact is enormous for that family, which in all likelihood is already struggling on the lower rung of the socioeconomic ladder. The families, the friends, the relatives of the incarcerated individual are all affected, and their problems spread into the wider community and still further into the society at large. It may well be that the membership of CFROP is a reflection of this reality, for the membership itself comprises a cross-section of society. There are, of course, the friends and relatives of prisoners, but also there are lawyers, teachers, business professionals, social workers, professors, college students, who all come together to help create the resources, the means, and the voice to change the conditions that victimize the poor.

Fostering awareness and education across the stratum of society is basic to the work of CFROP. The organization facilitates an understanding of how the socioeconomic structure of the larger society is connected with what is now known as the prison-industrial complex, in which both race and class are deeply embedded. "Few Americans are aware of the social costs, from the criminalization of a generation to the draining of

14. Reiman, *Rich Get Richer*, 119.

funds from education and social services, and fewer still are aware of the social forces driving prison expansion, particularly the use of prisons as a form of 'economic development' for poor rural communities."[15]

Not only have prisons become a facet of economic development for poor rural communities, they have also become a facet of economic development for the corporations comprising American society. Prisoners are now employed at slave wages, sometimes for as little as fifty cents an hour to produce goods such as contemporary sportswear for companies such as Eddie Bauer, allowing those at the top to gain huge monetary profits at the expense of those incarcerated.

When one considers the fact that not only are the majority of prisoners poor, but also that they are disproportionately African American, one has to consider the Thirteenth Amendment to the United States Constitution, which states that "neither slavery nor involuntary servitude, *except* as punishment for crime, whereof the party shall have been duly convicted, shall exist within the United States," as means of providing legitimacy for enslaving hundreds of thousands of African Americans within the confines of United States prisons. For as Harold Adams notes, "The unequal enforcement of the criminal laws in poor, largely minority neighborhoods in our nation's major cities has provided a loophole to make the Thirteenth Amendment inapplicable to the very grouping within our society who were previously held as chattel slaves and toward whom the Thirteenth Amendment abolition was purportedly directed."[16] The truth of this is disturbing as it should be. Well over a quarter of a century since the height of the civil rights movement, most Americans would like to believe that, for the most part, issues of racism in this country have been resolved. However, within the prison system issues of race are impossible to ignore for, "the United States' remarkable number and percentage of persons locked up by the state or otherwise under the watchful eye of the criminal justice authorities—far beyond those of the rest of the industrialized world—is black to an extraordinary degree."[17] It would seem that this issue is a vitally important one for congregational prison ministries to address, taking direct action to increase awareness both in their faith communities and the larger community as well.

15. Pranis, "Campus Activism," 158.

16. Adams, "Criminal Risk Factor," 2.

17. Street, "Color Bind," 31–32.

CFROP: A Path for Prison Ministry

Indeed, the Committee of Friends and Relatives of Prisoners can be a path for prison ministry within the church, for the church has always preached justice and mercy, has always upheld the care of the poor. While at times throughout the history of the church such solidarity and support has been perhaps more in word than in deed, nevertheless, it is the words and actions of Jesus of Nazareth that must necessarily provide the cornerstone for Christian witness. For truly, both his living and dying were all about justice and mercy, were all about the care of the poor. The scholar Obery M. Hendricks Jr. reminds us:

> We must never forget that, in large measure, it was against grave disparities in wealth that Jesus struggled and strove and preached and proclaimed God's judgment. Jesus taught that all God's children should live together in love and fellowship. A society built on the maintenance of social and economic classes stands in the way of the development of Jesus' beloved community.[18]

With millions of our sisters and brothers in the United States of America now imprisoned and with millions more affected by their imprisonment, the mission of the Committee of Friends and Relatives of Prisoners provides voice and witness, words and action for the creation of that beloved community.

CFROP's Benefit Program

Essential to the framework of CFROP is their cooperative networking Benefits Program, which helps to dismantle the sense of alienation and powerlessness faced by prisoners and their families and instead fosters a sense of connection and empowerment. The following benefits are provided by CFROP:

PRISONER NEEDS

With the privatization of prisons, prisoners in Massachusetts can no longer receive packages from family and friends with basic personal supplies such as toiletries, stamps, and nutritious foods to supplement the less-than-satisfactory prison diet. However, many families cannot afford to send the money to deposit into the prisoner's personal account so that they may buy the necessary items from the prison canteen. CFROP

18. Hendricks, *Politics of Jesus*, 278.

helps to organize supportive individuals to sponsor prisoners who have no such resources.

PRISON AND JAIL MESSAGE CENTER AND HOTLINE

CFROP maintains a twenty-four-hour message center and hotline to accept collect calls free of charge for prisoners who have or may have lost contact with their families due to evictions, a move, or loss of home phone service, as well as to deal with prisoners' inability to reach legal resources in emergencies or unresolved health problems. This benefit provides prisoners with a vitally important connection and helps to build a sense of community between prisoners and their families.

PEN PAL CORRESPONDENCE

With loneliness and isolation being one of the greatest problems that prisoners face, CFROP locates volunteers who through letter writing help to create positive bonds between prisoners and the outside community.

PRISON CORRESPONDENCE POSTAGE

As many family members and friends cannot afford postage, CFROP provides stamps to members who bring their letters written to prisoners in self-addressed, sealed envelopes. CFROP also provides special occasion cards donated from supportive individuals and organizations.

DOCUMENT ADVOCACY

There can often be administrative forms necessary for communication and access to prisoners, and CFROP assists friends and relatives of prisoners to obtain, complete, and submit such forms.

INFORMATION AND REFERRAL

Resource and referral listings are maintained and updated by CFROP with information as to how to find them, how to access them, and which are reliable.

HOSPITALITY HOSTS

As more and more prisoners are located far outside the greater Boston area, necessitating an overnight stay for family members, CFROP is organizing supportive individuals and organizations in areas near prisons to donate overnight housing.

Inside/Outside, CFROP's newsletter

A quarterly membership newsletter provides updated information on needs and issues of concern to the membership, with news of organizational events and programs.

Transportation

A real obstacle for friends and families of prisoners is transportation to the facility where the prisoner is located. With more and more prisons located in remote areas with little or no public transportation, the cost to travel back and forth can be extremely expensive. CFROP has organized volunteers to drive family and friends of prisoners to the prisons, and this too helps enormously to break down the isolation and powerlessness engendered by the prison system.

A Volunteer's Experience with CFROP

The story of Michael, a transportation volunteer may provide the clearest witness of how advantageous the transportation benefit can be in the midst of the harsh, bureaucratic, illogical, impersonal, and mechanical functioning of the Department of Corrections. For a few months, Michael had provided weekly transportation to Janice, a middle-aged woman who was visiting her terminally ill husband, who had been incarcerated for seventeen years. At the time Michael began driving Janice to visit her husband Billy in a prison facility fifty miles outside of the city, Billy had been diagnosed with cancer. The diagnosis was long in coming, as it had been months that Billy had complained of back pain only to be told it was sciatica. However, when the time came when Billy could no longer get out of bed, diagnostic studies revealed a tumor that had grown so large it had fractured his spine. Now Billy was scheduled for surgery. The growth of the tumor was so extensive that two operations were required, and following the second operation, Billy developed an infection so that he could not immediately begin chemotherapy but instead was returned to the prison facility.

While in the hospital, his wife Janice had encountered more than one barrier as she attempted to make contact with the doctor for information on the operation and Billy's prognosis. She learned that prisoners are listed on hospital patient information lists only as "John Doe" and no information is provided to relatives. As she tried to maneuver around such obstacles she was accused of trying to break the rules.

After Billy's return to the prison, on one particular Saturday, Michael drove Janice out to the facility for her visit. She did not think it was necessary for Michael to wait around so he agreed to return at 3:30 in the afternoon. However, when Janice signed in for her visit, she was told that Billy was not there, that no one knew where he was, nor was there anyone available to give her this information. With no way to contact Michael, she had no choice but to wait for his return several hours later.

The following day Janice was able to learn that Billy had been transferred to a hospital ICU unit that was managed by the Department of Corrections. To her dismay she was informed that prisoners transferred there were not allowed to have visitors for three weeks. The officer stated that his only responsibility was to inform Janice of Billy's death.

With the support of CFROP, however, contact was made with a state legislator who did facilitate Janice's visit to her husband. However, when their sons arrived to visit, they were denied because of their own previous history of incarceration. When they objected on the basis of their father's terminal illness they were threatened with arrest. Billy died two days later.

While Janice had informed the prison officials that she did not want an autopsy to be performed, when the funeral director arrived at the hospital to transport the body, he was informed that the body was not there nor did they know where the body was. Once again, Janice faced repeated obstacles as she tried to locate her husband's body. After numerous phone calls to reach the superintendent and being denied access to speak to him, she finally was able to talk directly with him, stating, "You have lost my husband's body!" Eventually, after being placed on hold for a quarter of an hour, she was told that the body was at the coroner's office for an autopsy, despite her specific instructions that no autopsy be performed. After Janice called the coroner herself to inform him that there was to be no autopsy, Billy's body was released to the funeral director.[19]

As a CFROP transportation volunteer, Michael played a significant part in this family's encounter with the Department of Corrections as they attempted to maneuver through the system at this difficult and emotionally painful time in their life. Undoubtedly, CFROP's presence,

19. Carey, "In Sickness and in Health," 15.

support, and advocacy made an unbearable situation just a little less intolerable. All so often, knowing that we are not alone, knowing that others do care is all that is necessary to uphold us and bring us through the darkest of times.

THE VALUE OF PEOPLE POWER

In his book, *Engaging the Powers*, Walter Wink acknowledges the value of power in "people power" to redress injustice, simultaneously noting that the power of the people "is still in its infancy."[20] In a similar manner, Bill Moyers, long-time public television host, in his address to Occidental College in Los Angeles, speaking of the widening gap between the rich and the poor, and the potent transfer of control and power to America's elite asks,

> What's to be done?
>
> The only *answer* to organized money is *organized* people.

Again:

> The only answer to organized money is *organized* people.

And again:

> The *only* answer to organized money is *organized* people.[21]

With the growing numbers of American citizens in bondage to a prison system that creates profit for a few at the expense of millions, whose crime, in a very real sense, is poverty, CFROP's mission of educating and empowering people on the inside and people on the outside, uniting them together in the movement of the great arc of the universe as it bends toward justice,[22] may indeed be a means of growing people power out of its infancy. Additionally, by means of its systemic organization of people, it may be one of the most hopeful answers in the face of the present prison-industrial complex.

That the church has a responsibility to engage in the work of prison ministry, there can be no doubt. The three models offered here are simply three possibilities for engaging in prison ministry. There are many

20. Wink, *Engaging the Powers*, 252.

21. Bill Moyers, "Time for Anger" (speech, Occidental College, Los Angeles, CA, February 7, 2007).

22. King, "*Where Do We Go?*" 252.

others to be explored and discovered. In his book, *An Expensive Way to Make Bad People Worse,* author (and prisoner), Jens Soering notes that

> In 2001, America's 134 mainline Christian denominations had 317,580 houses of worship. If each congregation "adopted" just two of the 625,000 inmates released from prison each year, there might only be 6,250 recidivists (at TOP's rate of 1%[23]) instead of 421,875 real and technical violators (at the current national rate of 67.5%). That would starve the correctional monster of the flesh and blood it needs to stay alive.[24]

While it is important to acknowledge the value of the more common prison ministry direction of prison chaplaincy, this is not enough. If we hope to be truly effective, we must pursue our ministry with the awareness of all the complexities as they exist, historically, sociologically, politically, and economically, even if only in small ways, remembering the admonition of the Trappist monk, Thomas Merton,

> Do not depend on the hope of results. When you are doing the sort of work you have taken on, essentially an apostolic work, you may have to face the fact that your work will be apparently worthless and even achieve no result at all, if not perhaps results opposite to what you expect. As you get used to this idea, you start more and more to concentrate not on the results, but on the value, the rightness, the truth of the work itself. And there too a great deal has to be gone through, as gradually you struggle less and less for an idea and more and more for specific people. The range tends to narrow down, but it gets much more real. In the end, it is the reality of personal relationships that saves everything.[25]

In our congregational prison ministries, it is essential that together we become aware and remain aware; for it is together that we will find our sacred power to transform and to be transformed.

---

23. Soering, *Expensive Way,* 65. (Soering notes that in Detroit, the Prison Fellowship Ministries TOP Program has achieved reoffense rates of only 1 percent by means of churches "adopting" a released prisoner, whereby the prisoner is provided with a support network that helps the individual become a productive citizen).

24. Ibid., 91.

25. Merton, "Letter to a Young Activist," 52.

QUESTIONS FOR REFLECTION AND DISCUSSION

1. In what ways have the three models presented here provided new understandings regarding prison ministry?

2. In our prison ministry work, have we taken the time and invested the effort to understand the people we minister to in prison, their families, the complexity of their lives, and the forces that have shaped them?

3. Can we pause to consider that our faith communities and our ministries may possibly be, in the words of Martin Luther King Jr., "dry as dust?" See p. 103.

4. What would it mean for our congregation to "adopt" a released prisoner? See p. 134. Consider the lawyer's question to Jesus in Luke 10:29.

5. What aspects of the three models of prison ministry offered here might be most valuable in fostering awareness and empowerment in your own prison ministry?

Conclusion: Discoveries and Implications

Whether the thrust of the Bible is on retribution or restoration is not a marginal issue. The question is at the heart of our understandings about the nature of God and about the nature of God's actions in history. It is not an issue which Christians can avoid.

—HOWARD ZEHR, *CHANGING LENSES*

M Y WORK, MY MINISTRY, my reading, and my research in the context of this guidebook has unequivocally fostered my own awareness and empowerment with regard to punishment and imprisonment. My research into the history of imprisonment, and its development from the earliest times to the present, has allowed for an entirely new understanding of class hierarchies, power, and economics embedded in the institution of the prison system. In tracing its development over hundreds of years, I came to realize the paucity of our human understanding, of our ability to truly see and know what it is we are doing, and yet we speak and act as if we do indeed have all the answers when it comes to criminal behavior and punishment. To recognize the part that the church and Christians have played as the institution of the prison has evolved is cause for a degree of contrition and sorrow. To recognize the limited involvement and responsibility that the church and Christians now exercise in light of the present-day mass incarceration of millions of human beings, most of whom are poor, undereducated, underprivileged minorities, raises serious implications with regard to what our Christian testimony is really all about. Do we simply talk the talk or we willing to walk the walk, even in small ways?

Perhaps, the discovery that has had its greatest impact on me are the economic and political aspects so deeply entwined within the present retributive justice system. So often, we tend to see only the surface of things without really understanding the deeper realities below that surface, without taking the time to explore and examine, closely and carefully, the meaning and significance of our actions and decisions. As individuals, as Christians, as congregations, this may be our biggest failing and our greatest challenge. This, however, takes time and effort, and it may well make us uncomfortable as old and outdated attitudes and understandings are dismantled. James Gilligan notes that "a society's prisons serve as a key for understanding the larger society as a whole. One can use the prison system as a magnifying glass through which one might see what is otherwise less easily discernible in the culture—underlying patterns of motivation, symbolization, and social structure that determines the life of the community as a whole."[1] His analogy is not one to which we would like to give much attention.

To recognize that the ideal of American justice is merely that—only an ideal—and that in practice there is one kind of justice for the middle and upper classes of society and another kind of justice for the lower classes of society is a recognition that is not pretty or pleasant. It destabilizes our image of the country we live in and our professed values. What do we do with such recognition? If there seems to be no alternative, then we are simply left feeling disillusioned and angry. However, coming to understand restorative justice, not merely in an abstract way, but in its fullness and deeper philosophy and practices, has provided me with hope and renewed energy. It is time for congregational prison ministries to come to know and to claim their Judeo-Christian foundations through the implementation of restorative practices. By recognizing that "true justice is action well designed to move toward restoration of community on terms best serving the valid interests of all persons concerned,"[2] we can transform the system of retributive justice into a system of restorative justice.

Learning that our present retributive justice system holds symbolic meaning for our images of God, for our relationship with God, and for our practices of punishment towards our human sisters and brothers opens up an entirely new perspective from which to view retributive justice. It offers both an invitation and a challenge to reconsider and reinvent new images and metaphors for God so that our relationships with God, with self, and with others may be transformed into mutual

1. Gilligan, *Violence*, 185.
2. DeWolf, *Crime and Punishment in America*, 172.

relationships of care and compassion, of justice and mercy. To recognize that the present retributive justice system generates evil (evil understood as radical disconnection), which only serves to spawn still more evil and disconnection, makes it imperative for congregational prison ministries to seek ways to build restorative justice practices within their communities. Such a system of restorative justice must be "guided by the value of healing,"[3] for the values of healing and wholeness undergirded the ministry of Jesus. His intimate relationship with God, his "Abba," infused his life with the power of the Spirit, and out of this power he yearned to heal and make whole, to live and share this power with us so that we too might live and share this power with one another. As Carter Heyward suggests, "God is our Sacred Power in the struggle to generate more fully mutual relation, in which all of us, not just a few, are empowered to live more fully just and compassionate lives."[4] A system of restorative justice fosters mutual relation with self, other, and with God.

In fostering mutual relation, restorative justice emphasizes our humanity, which in turn nurtures our humility, whereby we can come to recognize that all of us fall short of the mark, that all of us stand in need of forgiveness. While even the best of us tend to minimize our transgressions, remembering to cultivate a spirit of genuine humility keeps us rooted in our own humanity and simultaneously keeps us connected to one another with care and compassion. My reading and research informed my own personal experience of needing to come to a place of forgiveness for deep, deep wounds inflicted, and it provided understanding and reassurance that forgiveness is not easy, and that it is a process that takes time, perhaps even many, many years. Coming to a clearer and deeper understanding of the African concept of *ubuntu*, I discovered that this concept has profound implications for individuals and congregations in their understanding of forgiveness as it relates to offenders, victims, and the larger community. As forgiveness was another cornerstone of Jesus' ministry, fostering a deeper understanding of forgiveness as a process, of what it is and what it is not, may assist congregational prison ministries in becoming more aware and empowered in their ministry to victims, offenders, and their communities.

The implications for growing in awareness and empowerment to foster healing and connection through compassionate witnessing are

3. Johnstone, "Introduction," 5.
4. Heyward, *Saving Jesus*, 55.

significant, for our awareness or unawareness interfaces with our sense of empowerment or disempowerment, which in turn directly affects our thinking, our behavior, and our ability to act or not to act. If congregational prison ministries are to witness effectively and powerfully to their Christian testimonies of care and compassion, of justice and mercy, of healing and wholeness, it is necessary to foster awareness of the realities of the present retributive justice system if there is to be any hope of transformation to a system of justice that is restorative. As Rebecca Todd Peters affirms, "People have to open their eyes to injustice before they can begin to imagine making justice."[5]

While the three models offered for congregational prison ministry are simply three ways for congregations to become involved in prison ministry in meaningful ways, those ways provide avenues for profound transformation of both individuals and communities. Certainly, I have experienced personal growth, enrichment, and transformation as I have participated in each of them. With increased awareness, I have felt greater empowerment as I continue my ministry in this sphere, even amidst its overwhelming complexities. The complexities of the present retributive justice system undoubtedly seem intractable, and it is all too easy to despair, simply throwing one's hands up in defeat. However, to grow in awareness, to consider the problem from a new perspective, from a wider and deeper perspective, offers the hope of finding a new direction. As noted by Jim Consedine in his article, *Restorative Justice: Healing the Effects of Crime*, "We need to discover a philosophy that moves from punishment to reconciliation, from vengeance against offenders to healing for victims, from alienation and harshness to community and wholeness, from negativity and destructiveness to healing, forgiveness, and mercy. That philosophical base is restorative justice."[6]

Shifting from a practice of retributive justice to one of restorative justice calls for a shift in our attitudes and thinking with regard to punishment and imprisonment. Perhaps, it is possible that the present crisis in our prison system may be just one of the many crises that we are facing in our society at this time in history. Everywhere we look, all the many structures and organizations that have been the foundation of human civilization for centuries are disintegrating. It seems that everywhere we turn the institutions of government, education, medicine, the

5. Todd Peters, "Preparing Ourselves for Making Justice," 227.

6. Consedine, "Restorative Justice," 8.

economy, religion, the family, are no longer supporting or responding to the human community in all the ways they have thus far. While this naturally generates anxiety, uneasiness, and apprehension, it may be that we cannot yet see clearly what is looming on the horizon.

While most of us may not yet be able to see, others have been gifted with a deeper understanding and vision of the upheaval surrounding us at this time in human history. These are the postmodern prophets and one such prophet is, I believe, the priest and social psychologist Diarmuid O'Murchu, who believes that human civilization has entered a time of transition, revolutionary in scope. From the late Middle Ages, up through the Industrial Revolution, even until this present time, our world view has been rooted in a mechanical model of the universe; we have understood the world to be working as a great machine with all of its many parts, and our human structures and institutions reflect that understanding. However, with the unfolding of the twentieth century and most recently in the last several decades, with all the unprecedented advances in human knowledge and technology, this mechanistic worldview is no longer appropriate; it is no longer functional for the place to which we as the human species has evolved.

Instead, we are being called into a new worldview, an understanding of the world as a whole, with everything and everyone being interrelated. O'Murchu affirms, "It is a call to acknowledge and appreciate that everything (including humans) belongs to a greater whole; that all life forms are interdependent and need each other; that everything thrives, not in isolation and competition, but in mutual cooperation."[7] It seems to me that this is the very foundation of a theology of mutual relation; this is the very foundation of restorative justice where all participants— the victim, the perpetrator, the community—are seen as interdependent and that the healing of each is imperative for the healing of the whole. Indeed, the growing movement to a system of restorative justice may well be part of the larger transition and evolution in which we are immersed. The philosophical base of restorative justice does indeed call us to a transformation of our thinking, of our attitudes, of our practice towards our human sisters and brothers, to those who have been wounded and to those who have wounded others. We need not resist nor be fearful of such transformation, because this is what Jesus of Nazareth was all about, for as O'Murchu testifies, "The Kingdom that Jesus proclaimed

7. O'Murchu, *Our World in Transition*, 22.

is essentially about *transformation*: a new world order characterized by creative relationships of justice, love, and peace."[8] May this be *our* inspiration, in the early years of this new millennium, as we continue to grow in awareness and empowerment in our congregational prison ministries.

8. Ibid., 118.

Appendix

Resources for Prison Ministries, Prisoners, and Their Family and Friends

Aid to Incarcerated Mothers

434 Massachusetts Avenue, Suite 503
Boston, MA 02118
888-246-4302

Provides support to mothers who have had trouble with the criminal justice system.

Alternatives to Violence (AVP/USA)

1050 Selby Avenue
St. Paul, MN 55104
888-278-7820
avp@avpusa.org

Offers experiential workshops in conflict resolution, responses to violence, and personal growth through a nationwide and worldwide association of volunteer groups.

American Friends Service Committee Criminal Justice Program

2161 Massachusetts Avenue
Cambridge, MA 02140
617-661-6130
www.afsc.org

Provides education regarding the financial, human, and social costs of the present punitive system; seeks to support prisoner initiatives to effect institutional and personal change.

BOSTON THEOLOGICAL INSTITUTE

210 Herrick Road
Newton Centre, MA 02459
617-527-4880
btioffice@bostontheological.org

Offers programs on restorative justice.

BOSTON UNIVERSITY METROPOLITAN COLLEGE PRISON EDUCATION PROGRAM

755 Commonwealth Avenue, Room 35
Boston, MA 02215
617-353-6000
met@bu.edu

Offers the opportunity for rigorous study, which gives prisoners the intellectual leverage they need to revise their view of themselves and leave prison better equipped to contribute positively to their families and communities.

CENTER FOR RESTORATIVE JUSTICE

Suffolk University
8 Ashburton Place
Boston, MA 02108
617-305-1991
cri@suffolk.edu

Offers educational programs on restorative justice.

CITY MISSION SOCIETY OF BOSTON

14 Beacon Street, Suite 203
Boston, MA 02108
617-742-6830

Increases awareness about the critical need for policy reform and services through the Public Voice Project, a collaboration of formerly incarcerated people and prison advocates.

COMMITTEE OF FRIENDS AND RELATIVES OF PRISONERS (CFROP)

PO Box 240219
Dorchester, MA 02124
617-265-9689

Promotes self-help efforts to benefit families and friends of prisoners and their loved ones behind bars with the understanding that the problems on the inside have their roots in the problems on the outside.

COMMUNITIES FOR RESTORATIVE JUSTICE

219 Walden Street
Concord, MA 01742
978-318-3400

Partners with local police and citizens to foster restorative justice in the community.

CONCORD PRISON OUTREACH

PO Box 383
Concord, MA 01742
978-369-1430
Contact: Lenore James, director

A nonprofit volunteer organization that works cooperatively with the Department of Correction to help reduce recidivism through educational and personal growth programs, striving to prepare inmates for their return to society as responsible and productive citizens.

DEATH PENALTY FOCUS – CLERGY MOBILIZATION PROJECT

870 Market Street, Suite 859
San Francisco, CA 94102
415-243-0143
www.deathpenalty.org

Fosters awareness among clergy as to how to speak to their congregations about this important issue.

EX-OFFENDERS RE-ENTRY PROGRAM

Dorchester Temple Baptist Church
670 Washington Street
Dorchester, MA 02124
617-282-0155
www.exoffendersresources.org

Offers transitional services to people in prison, with support from representatives of six different faith groups.

LIONHEART FOUNDATION—NATIONAL EMOTIONAL LITERACY PROJECT FOR PRISONERS

Box 170115
Boston, MA 02118
781-444-6667
www.lionheart.org

Provides men and women in prison with an effective tool for rehabilitation and change through the publication and free distribution of the book *Houses of Healing: A Prisoner's Guide to Inner Peace and Freedom*, which gives incarcerated men and women throughout the United States powerful rehabilitative resources to help them interrupt life-long patterns of violence and addiction and start building productive lives.

MENNONITE CENTRAL COMMITTEE OFFICE ON JUSTICE AND PEACEBUILDING

21 South Twelfth Street
PO Box 500
Akron, PA 17501
717-859-1151
www.mcc.org

Offers restorative justice education and practice.

OUR PRISON NEIGHBORS

PO Box 3036
Acton, MA 01720
978-621-9213
www.ourprisonneighbors.org

Recruits, supports, and expands the role of volunteers in Massachusetts prisons, while seeking to deepen the understanding that we are all part of the same community.

PARTAKERS

230 Central Street
Auburndale, MA 02466
617-795-2725
www.partakers.org

Provides opportunities and support for prisoners to obtain four-year college degrees in prison; advocates for humane prison environments and sensible programs to promote accountability, responsibility, and rehabilitation; provides education and information on the prison system and issues of criminal justice and criminal justice reform.

PRISON BOOK PROGRAM

C/O Lucy Parsons Bookstore
1306 Hancock Street, Suite 100
Quincy, MA 02169
617-423-3298
www.prisonbookprogram.org

Supplies individuals and groups of prisoners with quality reading materials. With education the only proven tool to help prevent people from returning to prison again and again, literacy and access to reading materials are crucial for the personal, spiritual, and political development of all people.

PRISON FELLOWSHIP

44180 Riverside Parkway
Lansdowne, VA 20176
877-478-0100
www.pfm.org

Partners with local churches across the country to minister to a group that society often scorns and neglects: prisoners, ex-prisoners, and their families; reaches out both as an act of service to Jesus Christ and as a contribution to restoring peace to our cities and communities endangered by crime, believing that truly restorative change comes only through relationship with Jesus Christ.

PRISONERS RE-ENTRY WORKING GROUP

578 Massachusetts Avenue
Boston, MA 02118
617-236-1808
Contact: Carol Streiff

Publishes *Coming Home: A Resource Directory for Ex-Offenders Returning to Greater Boston Communities.*

Side by Side Community Circle

United Baptist Church
322 Centre Street
Jamaica Plain, MA 02130
617-780-5062

Offers a supportive community for formerly incarcerated family and friends.

Span Inc.

105 Chauncy Street
Boston, MA 02111
617-423-0750
info@spaninc.org

Assists people who are or have been in prison to achieve healthy, productive, and meaningful lives.

Spiritual Recovery for Wounded Soldiers

Greater Love Tabernacle
101 Nightingale Street
Dorchester, MA 02124
800-786-7094

Provides support groups for male and female ex-offenders.

United Souls Support Group

First Church in Roxbury
10 Putnam Street
Roxbury, MA 02119
617-445-8393

Provides support for men who are facing incarceration, currently incarcerated, or have been incarcerated.

Bibliography

Adams, Harold. "When Social-Economic Condition Equals Criminal Risk Factor." *InsideOutside* 1, no. 1 (2006): 2, 10, 14.

Allard, Pierre, and Wayne Northey. "Christianity: The Rediscovery of Restorative Justice." In *The Spiritual Roots of Restorative Justice*, edited by Michael L. Hadley, 119–41. Albany: State University of New York Press, 2001.

Ansbro, John J. *Martin Luther King, Jr.: The Making of a Mind*. Maryknoll, NY: Orbis Books, 1982.

Augsburger, David. *Helping People Forgive*. Louisville, KY: Westminster John Knox, 1996.

AVP/USA. *Alternatives to Violence Project Manual: Basic Course*. Plainfield, VT: AVP Distribution Service, 2002.

Bass, Dorothy C., ed. *Practicing Our Faith*. San Francisco: Jossey-Bass, 1997.

Battle, Michael. *Reconciliation: The Ubuntu Theology of Desmond Tutu*. Cleveland, OH: Pilgrim, 1997.

Bazemore, Gordon, and Mara Schiff, eds. *Restorative Community Justice: Repairing Harm and Transforming Communities*. Cincinnati, OH: Anderson, 2001.

Bazemore, Gordon, and Mark Umbreit. "A Comparison of Four Restorative Conferencing Models." In *A Restorative Justice Reader*, edited by Gerry Johnstone, 225–43. Portland, OR: Willan, 2003.

Blomberg, Thomas G., and Karol Lucken. *American Penology: A History of Control*. New York: Aldine De Gruyter, 2000.

Braithwaite, John. "Does Restorative Justice Work?" In *A Restorative Justice Reader*, edited by Gerry Johnstone, 320–52. Portland, OR: Willan, 2003.

Braithwaite, John. "Restorative Justice and a Better Future." In *A Restorative Justice Reader*, edited by Gerry Johnstone, 83–97. Portland, OR: Willan, 2003.

Burton-Rose, Daniel, ed. *The Celling of America*. Munroe, ME: Common Courage, 1998.

Carey, Michael. "In Sickness and in Health, 'Til Death Do Us Part.'" *InsideOutside* 1, no. 1 (2006): 7, 15.

Cayley, David. *The Expanding Prison*. Toronto: House of Anansi, 1998.

Chang-Muy, Fernando. "Detention of Migrants." In *Building Violence*, edited by John P. May, 100–104. Thousand Oaks, CA: Sage, 2000.

Chidester, David. *Christianity: A Global History*. San Francisco: Harpers, 2000.

Chinula, Donald. *Building King's Beloved Community*. Cleveland, OH: United Church, 1997.

Consedine, Jim. *Restorative Justice: Healing the Effects of Crime*. Lyttelton, New Zealand: Ploughshares, 1995, 11. Quoted in Hadley Michael L., ed., Introduction to *The Spiritual Roots of Restorative Justice* (Albany: State University of New York Press, 2001), 8.

Countryman, William L. *Forgiven and Forgiving*. Harrisburg, PA: Morehouse, 1998.

Couper, David. "Forgiveness in the Community: Views from an Episcopal Priest and Former Chief of Police." In *Exploring Forgiveness*, edited by Robert D. Enright and Joanna North, 121–30. Madison: University of Wisconsin Press, 1998.

Debs, Eugene. *Walls and Bars*. Chicago: Charles H. Kerr, 2000.

de Gruchy, John W. *Reconciliation: Restoring Justice*. Minneapolis, MN: Augsburg, 2002.

de Waal, Esther. *Seeking God: The Way of St. Benedict*. Collegeville, MN: Liturgical Press, 1984.

DeWolf, L. Harold. *Crime and Punishment in America*. New York: Harper & Row, 1975.

Dillard, Annie. *Teaching a Stone to Talk*. New York: Harper-Collins, 1982, 94–95. Quoted in Parker J. Palmer, *Let Your Life Speak* (San Francisco: Jossey-Bass, 2000), 80.

Dixon, Valerie. "Christian Ethics." Lecture, Andover Newton Theological School, Newton, MA, October 28, 2002.

Dow, Mark. "Secrecy, Power, Indefinite Detention." In *Prison Nation*, edited by Tara Herivel and Paul Wright, 93–99. New York: Routledge, 2003.

Meister Eckhart. In *Peacemaking Day by Day*. Erie, PA: Pax Christi USA, 1985.

Ellis, George F. R. "Exploring the Unique Role of Forgiveness." In *Forgiveness and Reconciliation*, edited by Raymond G. Helmick, S. J., and Rodney L. Petersen, 385–400. Radnor, PA: Templeton Foundation, 2001.

Enright, Robert D. *Forgiveness Is a Choice*. Washington, DC: American Psychological Association, 2001.

Enright, Robert D., and Joanna North, eds. *Exploring Forgiveness*. Madison: University of Wisconsin Press, 1998.

Foucault, Michel. *Discipline and Punish: The Birth of the Prison*. New York: Vintage, 1995.

Fowler, James. *Faithful Change*. Nashville, TN: Abingdon, 1996.

Gilligan, James. *Violence: Reflections on a National Epidemic*. New York: Vintage Books, 1996.

Gobodo-Madikizela, Pumla. *A Human Being Died That Night*. Boston: Houghton-Mifflin, 2003.

Goleman, David. *Emotional Intelligence*. New York: Bantam, 1995.

Govier, Trudy. *Forgiveness and Revenge*. London: Routledge, 2002.

Hadley, Michael L., ed. *The Spiritual Roots of Restorative Justice*. Albany: State University of New York Press, 2001.

Harrison, Beverly Wildung. *Justice in the Making*. Louisville, KY: Westminster John Knox, 2004.

Hanh, Thich Nhat. *Teachings on Love*. Berkeley, CA: Parallax, 1998.

Hedges, Chris. *Losing Moses on the Freeway: The Ten Commandments in America*. New York: Free Press, 2005.

Helmick, Raymond G., S. J., and Rodney L. Petersen, eds. *Forgiveness and Reconciliation*. Radnor, PA: Templeton Foundation, 2001.

Hendricks, Obery M., Jr. *The Politics of Jesus*. New York: Doubleday, 2006.

Herivel, Tara. "Wreaking Medical Mayhem on Women Prisoners in Washington State." In *Prison Nation: The Warehousing of America's Poor*, edited by Tara Herivel and Paul Wright, 174–80. New York: Routledge, 2003.

Herivel, Tara, and Paul Wright, eds. *Prison Nation*. New York: Routledge, 2003.

Herman, Judith. *Trauma and Recovery*. New York: Basic Books, 1997.

Heyward, Carter. *God in the Balance*. Cleveland: Pilgrim, 2002.

———. *Our Passion for Justice.* New York: Pilgrim, 1984.

———. *The Redemption of God.* Lanham, MD: University Press of America, 1982.

———. *Saving Jesus from Those Who Are Right.* Minneapolis, MN: Fortress, 1999.

hooks, bell. *Where We Stand: Class Matters.* New York: Routledge, 2000.

Johnstone, Gerry, ed. *A Restorative Justice Reader.* Portland, OR: Willan, 2003.

Jones, L. Gregory. "Forgiveness." In *Practicing Our Faith,* edited by Dorothy C. Bass, 133–47. San Francisco: Jossey Bass, 1997.

Jordan, Judith, et al. *Women's Growth in Connection.* New York: Guilford, 1991.

Kennedy, Robert F. "Day of Affirmation." Speech, University of Capetown, South Africa, June 6, 1966.

King, Coretta Scott. *The Words of Martin Luther King, Jr.* New York: Newmarket, 1996.

King, Martin Luther, Jr. "An Experiment in Love." In *A Testament of Hope: The Essential Writings and Speeches of Martin Luther King Jr.,* edited by James M. Washington, 16–20. New York: Harper Collins, 1986.

King, Martin Luther, Jr. *Strength to Love.* Philadelphia: Fortress, 1963.

King, Martin Luther, Jr. "A Testament of Hope." In *A Testament of Hope: The Essential Writings and Speeches of Martin Luther King Jr.,* edited by James M. Washington, 313–30. New York: Harper Collins, 1986.

King, Martin Luther, Jr. "Where Do We Go From Here?" In *A Testament of Hope: The Essential Writings and Speeches of Martin Luther King Jr.,* edited by James M. Washington, 245–52. New York: Harper Collins, 1986.

Kramer, Samuel Noah. *History Begins at Sumer.* New York: Doubleday, 1959. Quoted in Karl Menninger, *The Crime of Punishment* (New York: Viking, 1969).

LaCugna, Catherine Mowry. *God for Us.* San Francisco: Harper, 1973.

Lazare, Daniel. "Stars and Bars." *Nation,* August 27, 2007, 29–36.

Lewis, Michael. *Shame: The Exposed Self.* New York: Free Press, 1995.

Mackey, Virginia. *Punishment in the Scripture and Tradition of Judaism, Christianity, and Islam.* National Interreligious Task Force on Criminal Justice, 1983.

Magnani, Laura, and Harmon L. Wray. *Beyond Prisons.* Minneapolis, MN: Fortress, 2006.

Marshall, Christopher. *Beyond Retribution.* Grand Rapids, MI: Eerdmans, 2001.

Mauer, Marc. *The Race to Incarcerate.* New York: New Press, 1999.

May, John P., ed. *Building Violence.* Thousand Oaks, CA: Sage, 2000.

McFague, Sallie. *Models of God.* Philadelphia: Fortress, 1987.

McGowan, Randall. "The Well-Ordered Prison." In *The Oxford History of the Prison,* edited by Norval Morris and David J. Rothman, 71–99. Oxford: Oxford University Press, 1995.

McNeill, Donald P., et al. *Compassion: A Reflection on the Christian Life.* Garden City, NY: Doubleday, 1982.

Menninger, Karl. *The Crime of Punishment.* New York: Viking, 1969.

Merton, Thomas. *A Year with Thomas Merton.* Edited by Joanathan Martaldo. San Francisco: Harper, 2004.

Merton, Thomas. "Letter to a Young Activist." In *Peacemaking Day by Day.* Erie, PA: Pax Christi USA, 1985.

Metzger, Bruce M., and Roland E. Murphy, eds. *The New Oxford Annotated Bible.* New York: Oxford University Press, 1994.

Miller, Jean Baker, and Irene Pierce Stiver. *The Healing Connection.* Boston: Beacon, 1997.

Mitford, Jessica. *Kind and Usual Punishment*. New York: Alfred A. Knopf, 1973.

Morris, Norval, and David J. Rothman, eds. *The Oxford History of the Prison*. Oxford: Oxford University Press, 1995.

Moyers, Bill. "A Time for Anger, a Call to Action." Speech, Occidental College, Los Angeles, CA, February 7, 2007.

Muller-Fahrenholz, Geiko. *The Art of Forgiveness*. Geneva, Switzerland: WCC, 1997.

Myers, Ched. *The Biblical Vision of Sabbath Economics*. Washington, DC: Church of the Savior, 2001.

O'Murchu, Diarmuid. *Our World in Transition*. New York: Crossroad, 1995.

Pax Christi USA, *Peacemaking Day by Day*. Erie, PA: Pax Christi USA, 1980.

Peters, Edward M. "Prison before the Prison." In *The Oxford History of the Prison*, edited by Norval Morris and David J. Rothman, 3–43. Oxford: Oxford University Press, 1995.

Peterson, Eugene H. *The Message*. Colorado Springs, CO: NavPress, 2002.

Pranis, Kay. "Restorative Justice, Social Justice, and the Empowerment of Marginalized Populations." In *Restorative Community Justice: Repairing Harm and Transforming Communities*, edited by Gordon Bazemore and Mara Schiff, 287–306. Cincinatti, OH: Anderson, 2001.

Pranis, Kevin. "Campus Activism Defeats Multinational's Prison Profiteering." In *Prison Nation*, edited by Tara Herivel and Paul Wright, 156–63. New York: Routledge, 2003.

Reiman, Jeffrey. *The Rich Get Richer and the Poor Get Prison*. Boston: Allyn & Bacon, 2001.

Rothman, David. "Perfecting the Prison." In *The Oxford History of the Prison*, edited by Norval Morris and David J. Rothman, 100–116. Oxford: Oxford University Press, 1995.

Rotman, Edgardo. "The Failure of Reform: United States, 1865–1965." In *The Oxford History of the Prison*, edited by Norval Morris and David J. Rothman, 151–77. Oxford: Oxford University Press, 1995.

Saint-Exupery, Antoine de. *The Little Prince*. Translated by Richard Howard. New York: Harcourt, 2000.

Salzberg, Sharon. *Lovingkindness*. Boston: Shambala, 1995.

Schmookler, Andrew Bard. *The Parable of the Tribes*. Albany: State University of New York Press, 1995.

Schumacher, E. F. *A Guide for the Perplexed*. New York: Harper & Row, 1977.

Sharpe, Susan. *Restorative Justice: A Vision for Healing and Change*. Alberta, Canada: Mediation and Restorative Justice Centre, 1998.

Smedes, Lewis B. *The Art of Forgiving*. New York: Ballantine, 1996.

Soelle, Dorothee, and Cloyes, Shirley. *To Work and to Love: A Theology of Creation*. Philadelphia: Fortress, 1984.

Soering, Jens. *An Expensive Way to Make Bad People Worse*. New York: Lantern Books, 2004.

Spierenburg, Peter. "The Body and the State." In *The Oxford History of the Prison*, edited by Norval Morris and David J. Rothman, 44–70. Oxford: Oxford University Press, 1995.

Starhawk. *Truth or Dare*. San Francisco: Harper & Row, 1987.

Staub, Ervin, and Laurie Anne Pearlman. "Healing, Reconciliation, and Forgiving after Genocide and Other Collective Violence." In *Forgiveness and Reconciliation*, edited by Raymond G. Helmick, S. J., and Rodney L. Petersen, 205–228. Radnor, PA: Templeton Foundation, 2001.

Street, Paul. "Color Bind: Prisons and the New American Racism." In *Prison Nation*, edited by Tara Herivel and Paul Wright, 30–40. New York: Routledge, 2003.

Surrey, Judith. "Relationship and Empowerment." In *Women's Growth in Connection*, edited by Judith Jordan, et al., 162–80. New York: Guilford, 1991.

Thurman, Howard. *Jesus and the Disinherited*. Boston: Beacon, 1976.

Todd Peters, Rebecca. "Preparing Ourselves for Making Justice." In *Justice in the Making*, edited by Beverly Wildung Harrison, 226–28. Louisville, KY: Westminster John Knox, 2004.

Tutu, Desmond. *Hope and Suffering*. Grand Rapids, MI: Eerdmans, 1984.

———. *No Future without Forgiveness*. New York: Doubleday, 1999.

Washington, James M., ed. *A Testament of Hope: The Essential Writings and Speeches of Martin Luther King Jr.* New York: Harper Collins, 1986.

Weingarten, Kaethe. *Common Shock*. New York: New American Library, 2003.

———. "Witnessing, Wonder, and Hope." *Family Process* 39, no.4 (Winter 2000): 389–402.

Wheatley, Margaret. *Leadership and the New Science*. San Francisco: Berrett-Koehler, 1999.

Whitman, James Q. *Harsh Justice*. New York: Oxford University Press, 2003.

Williams, Delores S. *Sisters in the Wilderness*. New York: Maryknoll, 1993.

Wink, Walter. *Engaging the Powers*. Minneapolis, MN: Fortress, 1992.

———. *Naming the Powers*. Philadelphia: Fortress, 1984.

———. *The Powers That Be: Theology for a New Millennium*. New York: Doubleday, 1998.

Worthington, Everett L., Jr. "The Pyramid Model of Forgiveness: Some Interdisciplinary Speculations about Unforgiveness and the Promotion of Forgiveness." In *Dimensions of Forgiveness*, edited by Everett L. Worthington Jr., 107–138. Radnor, PA: Templeton Foundation, 1998.

Worthington, Everett L., Jr., ed. *Dimensions of Forgiveness*. Radnor, PA: Templeton Foundation, 1998.

Zehr, Howard. *Changing Lenses*. Scotsdale, PA: Herald, 1995.

———. *Doing Life*. Intercourse, PA: Good Books, 1996.

———. "Retributive Justice, Restorative Justice." In *A Restorative Justice Reader*, edited by Gerry Johnstone, 69–82. Portland, OR: Willan, 2003.

———. *The Little Book of Restorative Justice*. Intercourse, PA: Good Books, 2002.

———. *Transcending: Reflections of Crime Victims*. Intercourse, PA: Good Books, 2001.